* * *

"I first remember Daniel O'Leary sitting humbly in a crowd
of men at a male initiation rite I was leading here at rugged
Ghost Ranch in New Mexico.
Only when I talked with him and responded to his smile did
I realise I was meeting a very special human being.
"Only later did I realise how well known he was in the UK,
and more importantly how truly holy and good he was.
"Read even small parts of this marvellous book, and you will
know all of the same!"

Fr Richard Rohr, O.F.M.
Center for Action and Contemplation
Albuquerque, New Mexico

* * *

* * *

"Daniel O'Leary's life and priesthood were God's special gifts to His struggling people. We trusted Daniel. He understood our legitimate confusion and was generous to a fault in giving his entire life to helping us discover a loving, merciful God.

"Daniel was a theologian who knew God personally.

"He was a hero to me. Yet it was only in latter years we got to know each other better. We lived in two different worlds, both doing what we could to plant seeds of hope.

"Daniel came to The Graan in Enniskillen to talk at our Novena of Hope. We chatted our way through a couple of late nights. His incisive mind directed me away from the systemic failures of Vatican clericalism.

"We both accepted he could communicate with clergy more effectively than I could. He held that my gift was opening up an avenue of Hope for the unchurched masses.

"We spoke on the phone during his last few months on earth. He knew his time was short yet he laboured ceaselessly to finish this book as his last gift to us all. It was something he had to do before peacefully moving on to meet the God he came to know so intimately.

"During his final illness he was gifted with immense clarity about what is important and what is not. That is why this book is his greatest and his most inspirational. It is a fitting summation of his beautiful life."

Fr Brian D'Arcy, C.P.
Author, Newspaper Columnist and Broadcaster

* * *

DANCING TO MY DEATH

ALSO BY DANIEL O'LEARY

BOOKS:

Prism of Love (2000)

Travelling Light (2002)

Passion for the Possible (2003)

Already Within (2007)

Begin with the Heart (2008)

Unmasking God (2011)

Treasured and Transformed (2014)

The Happiness Habit (2015)

The Healing Habit (2016)

The Heavenly Habit (2017)

An Astonishing Secret (2017)

AUDIO:

Reaching for God's Light (2012)

Dancing

to my

death

with the love called Cancer

DANIEL O'LEARY

columba
BOOKS

First published in 2019 by

 **columba**BOOKS

23 Merrion Square North, Dublin 2
www.columbabooks.com

ISBN: 978-1-78218-362-4

Set in Linux Libertine 10/14 and Klinic Slab
Cover and book design by Alba Esteban | Columba Press
Printed by ScandBook, Sweden

* * *

"The most fortunate author is one who is able to say as an old man that all he had of life-giving, invigorating, uplifting, enlightening thoughts and feelings still lives on in his writings, and that he himself is only the grey ash, while the fire has been rescued and carried forth everywhere."

Friedrich Nietzsche,

Human, All too Human: A Book for Free Spirits.

* * *

CONTENTS

 # FOREWORD

Sr Stanislaus Kennedy

Daniel O' Leary's life and ministries were an incredible source of inspiration to hundreds of thousands of people right across the globe, right to the end of his life and beyond it. I, like many more people, met Daniel through his writings, his teachings, through his retreats and various other exchanges and each encounter with him was special. He was always encouraging, always challenging, incredibly empathetic; and his humility and his great kindness always shone through. His death in January 2019 leaves us with a huge sense of loss but it also leaves us with a deep sense of gratitude for the life he gifted us with, urging us all the time to live our lives more fully, more deeply, and more lovingly.

Daniel's life was a full one, he was literally full of life, and he shared that in every possible way he could with everyone. That included his gifts and talents as well as his vulnerability and his imperfections in a way that helped many people. For Daniel, God was an expansive God, a great God, a big God, a God of cosmic proportions, not one that we could confine to our thoughts, our ideas or our imagination, and certainly not to our institutions. Through all his writings and teachings, that was the God he drew us to. He wanted us all to know always that no matter what happened to us on our journey, no matter how much we felt we failed, we were eternally and unconditionally loved by our God who always and forever delights in us.

Daniel believed our fullest destiny was to become love in human form, to become fully ourselves. He knew that to become fully human is to become divine. He often cited the story of the prophet saying to the cherry tree, "cherry tree speak to me of God and the cherry tree blossomed" and so too with our lives, if our lives are to be divine, they must be fully human. Daniel reminded us again and again about the holiness of our hearts, about the wonder of our bodies, and the wisdom we carry within us. He wanted to reveal the intimate and liberating presence of the divine heart in our hearts, already waiting and hoping to be discovered at every moment and in every experience of every new day.

His whole life and passion was to help us realise as fully as possible the story of incarnation. God became human to reveal to us our divinity. Daniel found God in all of life and all life in God. In him there was no duality, there was no separation, everything is holy, everything one. In Jesus he helped us to find our own enfleshed God experiencing his humanity as we experience it. For Daniel the mystery of the universe is love, creation is of the order of love and God's love is the fundamental moving force in all created things.

One of Daniel's greatest gifts was his authenticity and his total honesty; he was able to share his light and shadow, his strength and weaknesses. Because of his deep inner life of prayer, he knew himself intimately and understood and accepted himself. He was able to share his life experience, his own humanity, his own struggles in a way that helped him relate in a very meaningful way with us in our search and in our struggles. Like Jesus he ministered from a position of vulnerability. But as well as sharing his weaknesses, failings and his vulnerability, he also shared his source of strength, and how he found strength in weakness and light hidden in the darkness.

During Daniel's last six months of life, he suffered intensely, physically, psychologically and spiritually. During those months he chronicled what was happening to him, the pain, the suffering, the darkness, but he also shared with great conviction what sustained him during that time and in this, his last book, *Dancing to my Death* we have this enlightened wisdom. He shared with us his experience of the cross but also his extraordinary faith and belief in the light within the suffering and the immense beauty that he knew awaited him. It is the story of faith, love and trust. This book is an extraordinary inspiration for everyone, but it is I think especially comforting for anyone encountering pain, suffering or darkness in their life.

THE WAY IT IS

There is a thread you follow. It goes among
things that change. But it doesn't change.
People wonder about what you are pursuing.
You have to explain about the thread.
But it is hard for others to see.
While you hold it you can't get lost.
Tragedies happen; people get hurt
or die; and you suffer and get old.
Nothing you do can stop time's unfolding.
You don't ever let go of the thread.[1]

The thread in this poem by William Stafford is your True Self. It is who you have always been, created in the image and likeness of Love. All you are called to do is nurture the love you are into a greater love so that it radiates visibly from you, like a sacrament called 'you'. Against this backdrop, death is no longer seen as a fearful enemy, but as part of our evolving world of love. It is a wild moment of growth and transformation into an unimaginable depth of being.

Daniel O'Leary

INTRODUCTION

Dear Reader,

This is a collection of some of my thoughts and feelings since I was diagnosed with cancer in June 2018. These no-frills reflections were written as they happened. Apart from some necessary editing in the interests of clarity and sequence, they remain essentially unaltered, with no attempt to justify or explain them; nor do they carry any 'messages' about a right way, or a wrong way to handle shocking happenings. Contradictions, mood swings and anomalies abound.

Please do not judge me; I have only risked writing the unbidden thoughts and feelings of my heart and mind. And please forgive me too; for the pathetic nature of my inability to cope with the cup I was given to drink. The pages resound with the cries of a self-centred 'poor me' victim, selfishly unaware of a wider and far more deserving world of indescribable pain outside my own. But that's the truth of these reflections. They simply describe what happened, and is still happening in my mind and heart.

But why write about them? I'm not sure. Maybe they will help my recovery and healing. Maybe not. Maybe, hopefully, they will comfort your own encounters with darkness. One thing I am sure of is how differently the mystery of one's life looks when viewed from the actual experience of shock, loss and the confusion of a routine that is suddenly up-ended and knocked utterly off track. It is a desperate place to be. When I am thrown into the water and cannot touch the bottom with my feet; when I'm hanging off the cliff-edge and can hold on no longer – then I panic!

These unframed, often barely connected meditations and reveries were written as they happened, covering a summer and an autumn. They are finally gathered together now in wintertime and will be with you in Spring 2019. And they are far from finished because they form the new setting, context and horizon for the remaining months of my life. Pillars of certainties, doctrines, teachings and religious habits have toppled. Foundations of my faith have been shaken. Raw experience takes no hostages to fortune. There is a silent assassination of shallow certainties.

I feel I need a bigger picture. The one I'm relying on is found wanting. Our God, our Faith, our Church are all just too shockingly small. The true Love that is God is beyond all religions, faiths and beliefs. Richard Rohr OFM writes that God is not only stranger than we think; God is stranger than we *can* think. And so, throughout these pages I have tried to outline and include glimpses of that bigger horizon of Creation and Incarnation, which you and I have patiently tried to share over the years and for which our hearts were created. That very wonder is keeping me from despair just now. Anyway, the rudderless confused drift of thoughts and feelings recounted in these pages is what happens when you lose your certainties and your True North. More deeply than I can say, I do appreciate your company, not only in the past in different ways, but during this current season of my bewilderment.

A thousand thanks.
Namaste.

Daniel.

Part One

❧ 1 ❧

RAW GRACE

Sincerest thanks, dear readers, for your support, encouragement and appreciation of my words, written and spoken, over the decades. You have been just wonderful. As I try to make friends with my new companion whose name is 'Cancer', there are many unformed and unfinished thoughts and feelings beginning to arise within me that I want to share with you, as I have shared with you before.

Over the decades my desire has always been to reveal to you something of the beautiful mystery of the God of my heart. Guided by the Holy Spirit, I hope that your hearts too may have been touched from time to time. Among the many inadequacies of my efforts, in the light of my current experiences of darkness and light, I am struck by the shallowness of much that I have said and written. My communication was mental rather than visceral; out of my head rather than out of my heart and guts; descriptive rather than personally expressive; not really hammered and moulded on the anvil of pain.

It isn't that my efforts were all wrong – they were just not shaped or uttered from a place of suffering and sacrifice. It isn't, either, that my efforts with you were untrue, or misleading – it's that they were cerebral rather than born of silence and suffering. Maybe that's the best I could do, at the time. A constant theme of mine, you may remember is the centrality of 'depth', especially in the manner in which Richard Rohr, one of my heroes, taught it. Now in my eighties, and the recent recipient of a cancer diagnosis, I am falling into an ambiguous, confusing and paradoxical abyss of unwelcome uncertainty. Well below the surface, my life is being radically changed: sometimes it's a terrible hell of darkness, sometimes a fleeting ray of dawn light.

My anticipation of this experience of dying seems very far removed from our conventional understanding of religion, religious practices, religious beliefs. It seems to have little to do with denominational differences, rubrics, orthodoxies, worthiness and infallibility. What's happening is like being stripped naked in public, where the ego is exposed in all its tricks of hiding, covering up, inauthenticity, falsity and fear. And even though it's early days yet, far too early to make sense in any definitive way, there are fleeting intimations, hints and guesses of many levels of darkness and love. I ask your permission to write about dark, raw and painful grace.

2

THE SPIRITUAL 'FIX'

Even on a good day, I cannot believe what people tell me – that this confusing time of anxiety in my life may yet offer the most potent moment for blossoming into my truest self, when the dream of my birth and baptism is realised, when the final break-through into the fulfilment of my being happens. Another pipe dream that mocks my diminishing faith. More often, just now, it feels like a condemnation of everything I hold dear, the death of my plans and desires, the unhappiest and most anguished time of my life. It is the time when I begin to realise, in all its starkness, the silent and invisible dominance and utter control that the ego possesses over my whole existence – the pervasive vanity in even those most inspired, holy and purest acts of service.

Imagine, for instance, something you dread – the inevitable diminishments of the senses in the process of getting old; the fear of the future and its unknown threats of serious illness; anxieties around being found out; the break-up of the family; the having to let go of everything you cherish; the fear and the panic of losing it all: losses more serious than our usual trials and tribulations. And we try all the faith-strategies and resources we know so as to survive and manage. Many of you have had Masses said for me, gone on pilgrimages for my healing, prayed incessantly for the shrinkage of my growing tumour. But a time comes when they do not seem to work. That time has now arrived for me. And it's all so real. You cannot argue with the truth of a tumour. Like a death knell it rings in your heart throughout the slow minutes, 'You have cancer and it has spread'. The grinning face of death becomes embossed on every new page of the mornings of my days.

And very occasionally, before the sun has set on another dull evening of another deeply troubled and grim day, I may glimpse a vague possibility, a blurred awareness, a graced chance of living at a radically different depth of awareness and experience of salvation, of seeing things, of coping with the confusion, fear and loss. This is a bigger challenge than ever before. I guess *I have to be* in this space of desperation before my heart's understanding can touch another level. Even in the most fleeting way. These insubstantial insights quickly disappear. As you will see, they swiftly come and go, an elusive golden thread to hang on to – and then the immediate loss of it. It is, of course, and will always be a slow journey. To avoid despair I find I have to keep trying to visualise a healing outcome, to imagine a new freedom, a more profound openness, a total trust, the deepest union with the Holy Spirit. This involves a constant vigilance and dedication to the work of converting my mind, heart, body and soul. And, just now, this conversion is most certainly not happening.

3

TWO WINDOWS

I must have spoken to you hundreds of times about trusting in God, about handing everything over, about a total surrender to Providence. So easy to say in theory; so impossible to do in reality when you are powerless to help yourself. The greatest suffering happens when we lose control over our future. Yet there is no option, as we've been saying for decades, but to surrender, to take that leap into the abyss – and to do it to the deepest degree. In seconds my mind's focus shifts between thoughts and emotions of despair and hope. Each day now is like looking out through one of two different windows – the usual current one onto a scene of hopelessness and threat; and, much more rarely, the other reveals the possible panorama of a new freedom and peace, where all control is relinquished. On the one hand, a frightening experience of fear and denial; on the other, a sense of the only and painful path to the authentic nature of my true self. *Deep in my heart, my loving Mother God, even for a nanosecond, help me to accept my life, my future, my death from your sure hands and heart.*

Both of these states of mind and soul come and go at every morning waking, at every evening silence, interwoven throughout each day, each hour. Ignatian spirituality speaks of desolation and consolation. It depends on which window I look through – the window of the wilful and fearful ego or the window of grace. And that choice is nearly always available – but is it a choice? I feel powerless in the face of the dark and desperate thoughts that arise within me. Sometimes, when I try to enter the pain, to breathe it in, the terrible fear retreats – just a tiny bit.

Don't turn your head.
Keep looking at the bandaged place.
That's where the Light enters you.[2]

There is no denying the anguish I feel. I know there must be much suffering and much loving going on in whatever is happening to me during this personal 'calvary'. 'This is it!' I say to myself – this, for me, just now, is the meaning of the saving and amazing grace of God, the abundant life. Can that be true? Sometimes however, and only in the vaguest of outlines, this confusing despair begins to lighten a little. 'Is this what the Christian story is about?' I begin to wonder. Am I in a vital moment of catharsis, of a detoxing of the false self, of an experience of facing the true self, of stripping down the masks, of a real form of inner death? Is this a moment of necessary grace, of understanding and actually experiencing a hint of redemption, of proving that 'I can do all things in him who makes me strong'? (Phil 4: 13). But can I?

4

TRUE NORTH

A few images may help readers to understand the shock of the 'bad' news. I felt I was living my life to the full, heading as faithfully and accurately as I could in the direction of my (and God's!) True North. It was what my life was about; what I had trained myself to do through study and reflection, the ministry I believed God wished for me, the vocation that was now a hundred percent of these later decades of my life. And I felt I was doing a good job; I was booked out; I had plans for another two books; my health was great; my barns were full.

Then one June morning in 2018, after a precautionary operation, it was as though a huge sign was flashed before my face: STOP! You're heading in the wrong direction. Your True North lies along another path entirely. According to God's compass you must start a completely new journey. You must re-think, re-adjust, re-calibrate your spiritual sat nav, re-vision every single thing you thought you already knew, and begin to die slowly into an equally slow re-birthing. It is called conversion. And it is the Lord who speaks. While your cancer is eating away at your vital visceral, destroying your very essentials for living, is something else within you taking shape?

There are many images in my mind and heart these days and nights. Too often, on early mornings, in a dream or a depressive reverie, I imagine myself in a neglected, musty, cobwebby, damp hut in the tangled woods. It is a place of no hope. The sky I love looking at, the rays of sun through the morning window, the twilight of magic – all gone. Only a shuttered window that keeps out the light and keeps in the fear. And then I hope, pray and imagine that one spring day some curious traveller will find the hut, force open the door, push through the cobwebs, and a small light will creep in, bringing hope and healing, beginning a slow transformation . . .

5

THE ABYSS

In every Eucharist Prayer, whatever the translation, just before the Consecration, we read about 'a death he (Jesus) freely accepted'. I have often lingered over these words. Especially now, in my own anxiety to turn back the clock. Even though cancer is no longer to be equated with death, old habits stay with us. How hard it is to say 'Yes Lord, I gladly accept this big cross. I surrender to it. I do know you neither will nor desire it for me. You cannot prevent it. But you can help me grow through it. Give me grace to accept this cancer which is devouring my life away.' Nor is there any hidden relief in saying those words and trying to achieve this understanding. The darkness does not shift; there is no light today.

Yesterday, reflecting on this stark reality, it suddenly occurred to me that THIS IS IT! Here is one of the lowest points of my life, and the dreaded despair of it. I'm in a place I've never been before. It's the moment we all fear most. Jesus too wept in that deadly experience of despair. And I, and millions each day, are there too. There is no other way to the abundant life, no other way for my divine and hidden self to come through. Right here and now is the abyss that has opened up for me, the abyss I knew awaited me but one I never expected to come in this searingly deadly shape.

THIS IS IT! For sure and for real. And my only hope is to welcome it, to hold it close to me, to actually strive to *experience* it: 'a death he freely accepted'. There are no ring roads around the desert, nor bridges across the abyss. Even the God of Love could not find one for a terrified and beloved son. Not merely a participant or observer any more – for him, for me, for millions of us. There is the need to *live and feel* the desolation, to visualise it, to experience the abyss of an endless falling. And can I, even for a moment, find some comfort in knowing that it cannot get any worse than this? That I'm as naked and vulnerable as I will ever be? That all I can do is enter more fully into that yawning cave, step by fearful step, breath by fearful breath, creeping ever more deeply into the unknown all-enveloping darkness?

❦ 6 ❦

PARADOX

What I am trying to do, in a more real and deeper way than ever before, is to make my wound into a sacred wound; to make the stones of darkness into welcome stepping stones of light across the turbulent river; to go through the pain to find the freedom that can only be found by doing precisely that. Many of you will maybe remember a few of the phrases, teachings, spiritual guidance that I've been working at since ordination nearly sixty years ago; but now they are assuming a totally new meaning and reality: the dying involved, the endless anxiety, and yet the confused awakening to another possibility. For it seems to me that if I lose this suffering of a sickening kind of darkness, I will lose the light too, on that very same day. It is no secret. Light and darkness, death and life can only live in each other's company. Something unbaptised and faithless within me rebels at this kind of thinking.

Pope Francis is never tired of emphasising the need for the actual EXPERIENCE of grace, of salvation, of 'calvary', of mercy. He, of course, had his own hell in his past life which was the foundation I think, of his remarkable vision into Incarnation now, and his relentless insistence on the necessity of practical love and compassion for the earth, for the poor, for 'the slightest speck of dust'. He often wrote and spoke of the paradox of the Christian life, the inbuilt contradiction of 'when I am weak then am I strong', 'when I'm lost then I'm found', when I'm experiencing cancer, then I'm experiencing a deeper way of living and dying. But every minute there is the temptation to return to, to weaken into, to fall back into the understandable but graceless way, the selfish self, the way of worry and doubt, the 'unspiritual way' of St Paul, the unredeemed and hopeless way. And who in their right senses would not understand that. Even Jesus had his times of doubt.

And at this moment these opposites move in and out of my awareness, as different as night and day, as darkness and light, as death and life, yet as intermingled as water and wine. Paradox and mystery in every minute: depth and emptiness, vision and blindness, freedom and desperation. Amazingly they need each other. We are well aware of the death in every birth, of the oneness of Good Friday and Easter Sunday. Without the dark and fearful struggle, the inner pain, there can be no meaning at all in our creeds, doctrines, sacraments and teachings. Pope Francis keeps repeating his criticism of the shallow and simplistic Christianity of so many Catholics.

7

INCARNATION

Once I no longer turn, in my pain, to a God 'out there' but reach within to the intimate presence of a God who lives in my heart and in the heart of the world, in my body and in the body of the universe, as Incarnation happily calls me to do, then the challenge of my encounter with cancer takes on a radically different and richer meaning. There will still be the shock, the initial denial, the paralysing fear, the anger; but my overall grappling with its meaning gradually, very gradually, makes some kind of sense. I'm given vague glimpses of the part my suffering plays in the suffering of God, of the persecuted, of the world itself in its evolution. It slowly becomes less my own pain only but a participation in God's universal and continuing agony too. This understanding of Incarnation tells me that in the enduring of my blind, blank night I'm somehow creating another troubled space for Christ to be born into the world, another small dawning of Incarnation, something to do with what is still lacking in the sacrifice of our Saviour.

What is happening to me is part of a bigger plan. I try to align myself with God's desire for all creation and for everyone in it. I try to let go of my own yearning for a healthy body, for a happy mind, for success, for a personal salvation. I'm hoping my soul will be renewed along different lines to the flawed spirituality of the past. I sometimes wonder if a unique, special and most powerful opportunity is being offered to me in my shock, my horror, my resistance. Is a new horizon about to emerge? Another way of knowing and following God's ways? Will a new way of being replace all I once considered as the key to holiness, but now realise was not enough? The *unum necessarium,* the one central and final surrender was still missing. Is that the whole meaning of what's happening to me now, a call to me to share the fate of the incarnate God for the life of the world?

Is this unwelcome visitation that has upended my carefully planned life, a revelation of what is genuinely mine to offer the world for its Spirit-led evolution into a future heaven? Is this shocking interruption of my 'clerical ministry' an indication of my neglect of the one reason I was born, so as to become the authentic 'me' that God wished for; a sign that I was utterly ignoring, pandering to the whims of my ego instead? The offering of that gift, my true self, is the ultimate gesture I can make to love and serve the world. Is that the meaning of those household words our parents would say to us as children (and in which, I'm afraid we found little consolation!) as we cried our pain – 'Offer it up!'

❧ 8 ❧

LET YOUR LIFE SPEAK

At eighty-one, is this, at last, the purpose of my life: to come to terms with the cancer and its spreading that I'm now living with? Is this the calling I've ignored for too long – the deep experience of diminishing, decaying and dying? Did I refuse to take time to go below the surface of my life? Referring to Jonah, Richard Rohr reminds us that "It sometimes takes being swallowed by a whale and taken into the darkest place to let go of our small, separate self and its private agenda". Is this what is now happening to me? Am I to be shocked out of my ego-life in order to follow my deepest soul's desire to let go, in trust, in a way I never have before? How severe the shattering moment must be before we are sufficiently broken enough to get the message, to seek and pursue our true identity in preparation for heaven! Do these thoughts ever cross your busy mind? Do you think they apply to you?

"There are moments (of utter shock)," writes Quaker Parker J Palmer, "when it is clear, if I have eyes to see, that the life I am living is not the same as the abundant life that I was born to live." St Paul rejoices when he writes, "I live now, not I; another Life lives in me" (Gal 2: 20). Palmer continues, "In those moments I sometimes catch a glimpse of my true life, my true self, a life hidden like the river beneath the ice. And I wonder: what am I meant to do? Who am I meant to be?" Even when following the loftiest ideals, Palmer realised that he was living life from the outside in, rather than from the inside out; a life spent "imitating holy heroes rather than listening to my heart".[3]

Does it take an experience such as mine to listen to one's true heart, to let one's truest life speak? Richard Rohr writes, "Your life is

not about you. You are about a larger thing called Life. You are not
your own. Life is living itself in you. The many forms of evolving
life in the universe are merely part of the One Life, what many of
us call God."[4]

9

LOST?

As I try to keep my heart up while coping with this sudden and unwelcome intrusion into my life, I realise that the Christian faith is not about worshipping Jesus, placing him on a pedestal higher than all others, endlessly proselytising for his glory and my own salvation. Most certainly it is not about devotion to the externals of religion, the belief systems of Christianity, the useless fuss about rubrics and regulations. It is more about *following* Jesus, offering my life to share the fate of God, like he did, for the peace and future of our evolving world. How can I transform my life, built on the image of God in which I'm born and baptised, into the divine likeness? We are all born, the Eastern Church reminds us, with that origin, calling and destiny. Like Blessed John Henry Newman in his time of trial, I ask myself what facet of the divine beauty I am called to reveal in how I accept and interact with the shattering experience of cancer during this diminishing season of my life.

All too easily we get cocooned in our private little lives of personal pursuits, in our ambitions and exclusive addictions to power, possessions and privilege. We can get lost in our inappropriate attachment to success at work, to the accomplishments of our children, to the acquisition of prestige in our community. We can get lost in our careers, in mid-life, in our suffering. Looking back now, I'm sure I was getting lost in the pursuit of my ministry of teaching and writing, forgetting that what mattered was the deeper understanding of my hidden Christ-self, the incarnate *becoming* of the challenging ideas I was dispensing all over the place.

Poet David Whyte wrote:

...Sometimes it takes darkness and the
sweet confinement of your aloneness
to learn anything or anyone
that does not bring you alive
is too small for you.[5]

I am asked to believe, in spite of all the evidence to the contrary, that the darkness of these days, weeks, months are bringing me to the threshold of a new wisdom. Yes, they say, there will be a painful dying. But also, they add, the birth of new and undreamt-of possibilities for the future. Yes, they say, there will be many Gethsemane nights of utter struggle. But also a silence for the whisper of the Spirit's ocean to be heard through the open window 'like a far wave'. Even Jesus was lost that night too, they remind us, in the garden before he could hear the comforting voice of his father in his breaking heart. And does everyone have to suffer these terrible experiences before discovering the meaning of intimacy with God, of 'the abundant life', of the 'True Self'? Do you? And are you ready?

❧ 10 ❧

GIFT?

There's a gift hidden in your new condition, I'm told. A special silver lining in your hungry cancer. Bright revelations emerging from your chemo sickness. But no! These are phrases I've used so often myself – truly believing them without ever experiencing them. If this emergence of graced insight be true (and mostly now I doubt it) then I pray it helps me understand and experience a little more of the mystery of unconditional love, the love that is the energy of Creation, the love that is the artistry of the Holy Spirit in Evolution, the love that reveals the utter intimacy of God's beauty in everything that exists, the love that changes everything. That would be something! And no signs of it yet! Just more wretched waiting.

That last paragraph springs from, and only from, a persistent belief in the physical fleshing of Love, in the divine presence that pervades everything in our lives. It is why I long to be more sure that we cannot love God unless we love the world, the body of God first. This is the forgotten heart of Incarnation. As Sally McFague reminds us, we are not called to love God *or* the world; rather are we called to love God the essence of the world. We love God by loving the world. We love God through and with the world. With all my heart I want to know, believe and become that life-giving wisdom. And to continue meditating on it for as long as I've got. There are not two ways of our loving, two recipients of it – one human, one divine. There's only the one love. Incarnation makes that clear. But that saving revelation was never passed on to us. And please don't wait for a tragedy to bring this home to you too!

So, my prayer is that this enervating experience which is consuming my energy will somehow provide the opportunity for deepening my grasp of the mystery of God's astonishing presence, source and sustenance of all life. Incarnation reveals beyond any argument, beyond the slightest doubt, that there is nothing that is grace-less. Christianity is grounded in that belief. We are working and playing intimately with God, already experienced in our every breath and heartbeat, as we follow our soul's calling, as we love everyone and everything, including sudden tumours and sudden tumults, as unconditionally as we can muster. With constant discernment, the true Christian rejoices in the almost unbelievable achievements of this technological age, in the stunning revelations of science, in the ever-increasing revelations of the love-energy and craftsmanship of the Holy Spirit. All of this is what I yearn to explore and adore. With Teilhard de Chardin I want to fall on my knees and say: *Lord Jesus, you who are as gentle as the human heart, as fiery as the forces of nature, as intimate as life itself, you in whom I can melt away and with whom I must have mastery and freedom: I love you as a world, as this world which has captivated my heart; and it is you, I now realise, that my fellow humans, even those who do not believe, sense and see through the magic immensities of the cosmos.*[6] The very sweep and swirl of that prayer, the space and freedom of it, the cosmic bigness and yet the personal intimacy of it – I think it must surely heal my tumour and my mind just before my world grows too dark.

❦ 11 ❦

ASTONISHING SECRET

Forgive me for mentioning the title of my recent book, *An Astonishing Secret*. This is not a cheap sales shot. I mention it at this most trustworthy moment of my threatened life only to emphasise the focus of my work, play and prayer, the core attraction of my soul for many years. Nor is this an educational on what engages my heart. Too late for all that. I just want to understand more clearly the astonishing heart of 'the Incarnation secret', and how it already infiltrates my current chaotic consciousness.

I find I cannot face or think about 'my' cancer without seeing it against the wide and wonderful panorama of all God's continuing Creation as it develops through the unfolding story of Evolution. And the story has only just begun. Everything about God, about life, about faith, about the future, about suffering, changes when we allow the vision of our best theologians, mystics and scientists to invade our hearts. Even when my mind is distracted a thousand times a day, it still keeps drifting back to the comforting and healing mystery of the implications of Incarnation. Even just *thinking* about it is an invisible therapy!

What do I mean by that? Well, whenever we equate God with life itself a transformation takes place in the way we understand our Catholic Christianity. (I beg of you, dear reader, do all you can to become familiar with these traditional, safe and sound sentiments of our faith. You will be drawn to them because your heart was made to be nourished by them. Forgive me for referring again to *An Astonishing Secret*.) Once we remove everything that separates divinity and humanity, heaven and earth, grace and nature, then we begin to truly and freely live and move in another milieu. Once we use the same name for the Gracious Mysterious Mother of all becoming that we call God, and the primal energy of Creation and on-going Evolution, our faith can never be the same again. And once we commit to identifying God's intimate presence in our evolving, sensual perception of the world's most beautiful artistry, creativity and imagination, in our very breath, in our darkness and invincible light, then we are living the incarnation of God in Jesus. This is not a vague spiritual insight; it is a kind of heart-wisdom, a soul-awareness that immediately touches the most substantial parts of us, that brings a kind of peace when the tumult seems unending.

And this is why I cannot pray to God to blast the tumour, to remove it from my body, to shrink it to a peanut overnight – because I believe God's own energy is somehow at work in that tumour: in its genesis, its spreading, its reasons for existing and its final accomplishment. "Blessed be you, mortal matter," writes de Chardin, "you who one day will undergo the process of dissolution within us and will thereby take us forcibly into the very heart of that which exists." What a wonderful prayer that is! Death is the only way through into the next evolution of life, of our own lives. "Without you," he continues, "without your onslaughts, without your uprooting of us, we should remain all our lives inert, stagnant, puerile, ignorant both of ourselves and of God. You who batter us and then dress our wounds, you who resist us and yield to us, you who wreck and build, you who shackle and liberate, the sap of our souls, the hand of God, the flesh of Christ: it is you, matter, that I bless."[7] It seems as though this practical mystic, scientist and priest, wants us to see ourselves as a tiny atom in the cosmic context of the Risen Christ, of a piece with all Creation, and in the wider perspective of an evolving world. "Such a person's life," he writes, "is open to larger horizons, and such a person's heart is always more receptive."[8] That is the kind of thinking, of meditation, of wondering that sets me free to turn over in bed these nights, to close my eyes in thanks, and to forget, for a few hours the waiting demons of dawn.

❧ 12 ❧

CANTUS FIRMUS

Reflecting on the *cantus firmus* (the enduring melody) of their lives has empowered many to avoid despair in their most testing times. The enduring melody of a life is its inmost conviction, a truth that's never doubted, the logo of the soul, a basic vision that may fade but never leaves one, that always, even though in glimpses, delights the inner being. What excites and sustains our souls throughout the varied seasons of our days, so often returns to us when the ghosts gather, when only a bleak and bare landscape faces us each morning when we pull back the blinds. This is what I rely on, lean on, draw on, during these ambiguous moments when I still long to wake up from a bad dream.

It is only when we find age, illness or death upon us that we begin to think about what has remained constant throughout the vicissitudes of our decades; what has coloured our uncertainties and doubts with the bright brush strokes of a kind of passion; what has guided our directions when lost, faithfully guaranteeing a True North for the compass of our souls. I like to think that my *cantus firmus* is that divine image we were all born with, confirmed beyond doubt by baptism, that evergreen soul that outlasts a hundred winters. For many of the heroes and heroines of my life, tempered and polished in the openness and curiosity of their imagination, there has been an abiding sense of wonder that I try to experience and share too. When I re-read my retreat notes and books just to make sure, there is no doubt about this fascination. And for me, the sense of wonder has always arisen from the Christian creativity around the magic of Creation and Evolution, as revealed by the Incarnation.

Those of you who have suffered my books and retreats may have some idea of what this enduring refrain might be. It will punctuate this book too. It has many names. Do not be put off by them – *a theology of Creation and Evolution, a spirituality of Incarnation, the 'catholic imagination', the sacramental approach* – in this book they all mean much the same! You will get a firmer grip on their meaning as you turn these pages. And really, it is all unbelievably simple! They can be studied for a lifetime as an introduction to the deep Incarnation (and this, of course, is what our best theologians do), or they can be fully experienced in a heart-instant, in the way we look at God's secrets strewn extravagantly around us, where the divine fingerprints are everywhere. I remember writing once that "nothing has ever been written by a theologian about the meaning of God's Incarnation that hasn't been better traced in the crystal calligraphy of a frosty morning window; nothing has ever been preached by saints about divine beauty and intimacy that hasn't been better sung by the summer wind in the roadside trees; and nothing has ever been created by the mystics about incarnate love and beauty that hasn't been more poignantly revealed in the sleepy eyes of a new baby".

As my tumour grows and my hope diminishes, I continue to reach out of the life-less place I'm in, for stronger, reassuring, comforting glimpses of the astonishing love and meaning in all that surrounds me. When everything we see, touch, hear and smell is perceived as the warm embrace of the divine arms; when the spring song of birth and the winter lamentations of death are enjoyed and endured as the evolving seasons of God's Creation; when the twinning of the New Universe Story and the old Christian narrative captures our hearts with a profound, transforming and permanent wonder; when the courage and hope of oppressed people on a mutilated Earth are experienced as the empowering presence of the Holy Spirit within; when, from the jaws of a rampant cancer someone draws a pencil-line of light into the darkness; then, and only then, are we living and dying the gospel of Christian Incarnation.

This long sentence, and those big words are not just brain fodder; they are a kind comfort for the heart and soul. They are part of the vision that sometimes allows me to escape from the harsh interrogation of sleepless twilight hours into this bigger and beautiful picture of which I'm one small but integral segment. It is safe to go to sleep to this cosmic song of the manger. Please reflect on what your *cantus firmus* might be. You may one day need it as I do mine now. Or St Peter might just ask for a look at it as your ID when you approach those Shiny Gates.

13

PERSPECTIVES

The shock and struggle of coming to terms with cancer brings profound changes to one's perspectives on reality. Awareness contracts. The world closes in. A breathing space of width and depth is lost in self-absorption. The universe shrinks to the size of the tumour. The soul may diminish to a pinhead. In the light of this I'm trying to keep my heart big, to stay open to the healing of the sheer immensity and magnanimity of everything – the sky, the sea, Creation, Evolution, the human heart, the heart of God, the heart of an insect, the expanding cosmos. And even the silent tumour is somehow a tiny element of all that, a necessary dimension of life and death, of becoming, of being a part of the bigger, beloved and broken Creation, utterly subject to the vicissitudes of Evolution. In this way I try, as I persevere with my contemplation practice, to offer my full cooperation to the inevitable.

What do I mean by that? One kind of devotion may interpret 'giving my full cooperation to the inevitable' as 'offering it all up to God', or 'obeying God's will', or 'God gives and God takes away'. People pray that 'God will destroy this monstrous cancer'; they offer Masses, undertake novenas and pilgrimages for me, so that God may perform a miracle. People of great faith, who pray for me in these ways, touch my heart deeply. These beautiful souls of such intense commitment are so totally on my side. They are driven by a non-negotiable force. My mother, a committed believer in miracles, had her special saints, who had the ear of the 'Creator Himself'! Hers was a fierce faith. That is the stock I come from too. Bare knees on a cold floor in front of the lit picture of the Sacred Heart as we rattled through the rosary, litanies and my mother's list of her favourite saints – and we never missed a single night.

There is, however, another kind of devotion that I now rely on. In the course of my life, my experiences, my study, my contemplation, I have learned to pray as I can, not as I should. Those of you who are familiar with the content, the emphases, the direction of my retreats and books, will have an idea of how I struggle to understand a little more of the mystery we are all a part of: the divinity of life, of Creation, of nature, of Evolution, of humanity, of all true love, of each nanosecond of every day. This is how I now try to pray, to be present, to meditate, to be before God as I hold my cancer to my heart. I try to remember that light is always stronger than the shadows – and to choose it; that life is always stronger than death – and to choose it; that a courageous openness is always stronger than a fearful closedness – and to choose it; that a trusting acceptance is always stronger than denial or refusal. My prayer is about this total acceptance of what is happening, what I believe to be the way of the Holy Spirit of Evolution, rather than any attempt to change God's will about this or that. There is only the utter surrender to the divine reality of the here and now. And my mother, given the challenges of her life, would most certainly understand that.

❦ 14 ❦

A BIG LOVE

Beyond the frantic obsessing about smaller and personal issues, contemplation-time, I find, somehow orientates the soul towards the bigger horizons where love seems to infuse everything. Contemplation unconsciously nourishes a deep surrender to the unfolding of life itself – its cancers as well as its gifts – because for the Christian, this is the only unfolding of God we will ever experience. Our deepest longing is to touch the love that lies at the core of our being, to be intimate with the love that infuses everything, to be held closely by the everlasting arms of the Creator called Beloved. We become more aware of these insights in the stillness of prayer, where all wisdom is already present, and where all questions lose their urgency. In my attempts at praying, except in my more anxious moments, I no longer ask my Creator to take the cancer away. The tumour is somehow part of the bigger picture of a loving evolution ordained by God. I try to believe that the only answer is the daily openness and painful surrender to becoming Love incarnate, Love made flesh. And, for the record, when I prayed during my life for this to happen, to become Love made flesh in me, how little I knew about the price involved – the acceptance of a slow and feared death now underway – a price indeed "costing not less than everything"[9]. If you dare to love, be prepared to grieve.

To soak myself in this bigger picture, this vision of Pope Francis' 'magnanimity' which includes the universal reality of decline and death, I try to pray as de Chardin prayed. Only the universe itself was big enough to fill the huge heart of the poet, priest and scientist: *Lord Jesus Christ, you truly contain within your gentleness, within your humanity, all the unyielding immensity and grandeur of the world... I love you, Lord Jesus, because of the multitude who shelter within you and whom, if one clings closely to you, one can hear with all the other beings murmuring, praying, weeping. I love you for the extensions of your body and soul to the farthest corners of creation through grace, through life, through matter.*[10] And through death.

In this way I try not to blame or be angry with God for the cancer that has already shattered my plans, and is already transforming my life as each day the truth of it all sinks in with a sickening feeling. I do not think God has 'sent' it for any holy reason, nor could God do anything to prevent it, but only cries when I cry. God is for life, for completion, for fullness, for abundant being: "To fully *be* – for this God created all; the world's created things have health in them; in them no fatal poison is found." (Wis 1: 14)

Beyond the debate about individual salvation, the winning of heaven with its everlasting happiness, an expansive Christian vision sees a necessity and value in all suffering. And I have a choice. Do I rail against the Creator for this untimely annihilation of all that life means to me, or do I reflect on the wider, deeper vision of a constantly developing Creation of Love, with the unavoidable, evolutionary dimension of wastage, death, evil, sin? There is no way I can avoid the consequences, the tragedies as well as the glory of the world of which I am an integral part. Out of my own pain I try to deepen, enrich, empower this understanding of the heart of my suffering.

✣ 15 ✣

SUFFERING?

When something like cancer explodes all your plans and purpose, when everything that makes life meaningful and worth living for you is suddenly blown away, when you find yourself lost in an utterly unfamiliar and terrible place, then many desperate questions clamour in your soul. Again I turned to the thoughts of the sublime and practical mystic Jesuit, de Chardin, and his understanding of the place and role of suffering in the evolving thrust of our lives, and that of the universe. He believes we cannot progress in our growing and evolving without paying "a mysterious tribute of tears, blood and sin".[11] As the darkness grows more intense, a light grows brighter. For him, suffering in all its forms and all its degrees, is no more than a natural consequence of a graced evolution. He wrote of "the spiritual energy of suffering". Like St Francis before him, he greeted death as a necessary family member. He believed, as a Christian, that suffering can be transformed into "an expression of love and a principle of union". He wrote: "Yes, indeed: suffering in obscurity, suffering with all its repulsiveness, elevated for the humblest of patients into a supremely active principle of universal humanisation and divinisation – such is seen to be at its peak the fantastic spiritual dynamic force, born of the cross."[12]

In my own pain I struggle with all of this. Yet I sense it is true. Suffering has a power to open up horizons of love that remain closed to all other human experiences. There are gates of mystery that open only to tears. Teilhard writes, "In suffering the ascending force of the world is concealed in a very intense form." We would remain blind and deaf to beauty, to courage, to astonishment, if we never suffered. He continues, "The world would leap high toward God if all the sick together were to turn their pain into a common desire for the kingdom of God..."[13] Inspired by the Incarnation, he marvelled at the mysterious powers of creation and evolution.

When I get lost in my current fears and despairing thoughts, the beautiful world I love fades away from me. Only the bigger picture keeps me sane, and enables me to keep some semblance of balanced perspective in my mind. I begin to believe that my 'freely accepted' suffering (as in the death of Jesus) plays a central part in the saving, flourishing and divinising of the evolving world! I quote Teilhard again: "Could it not be precisely for this that the creation was completed in Christian eyes by the passion of Jesus? We are perhaps in danger of seeing on the cross only an individual suffering, a single act of redemption. The wider creative (and cosmic) power of that death escapes us. With a broader and deeper insight we would meditate on the cross as the symbol and focus of an action whose intensity is beyond expression... It is here that Jesus is bearing the weight, drawing ever higher towards the final Omega, the universal march of evolution."[14]

Here am I, unknowingly, co-creating with God, like Jesus did, the slow emergence of an astonishing future. These thoughts, on troubled nights, bring some balm to my stalled heart. In *Befriending the Stranger* Jean Vanier writes: "It is important to enter the mystery of pain – the pain of our brothers and sisters in countries that are at war; the pain of our sisters and brothers who are sick, who are hungry, who are in prison; brothers and sisters who do not know where they will sleep this night. It is important to enter into the pain of all those for whom no one cares and who are alone, all those who are living grief and loss."[15] And I have always tried, in my own terror of any kind of pain, to pray especially for those who will spend the coming day enduring some form of torture – physical, emotional, mental.

And yet, dear reader, in spite of these sublime aspirations and motivations, in my frequent moments of raw pain, something within me often screams in desperation; 'My God, my God, where the hell have you gone, what kind of game are you playing, you false and fine-weather friend?'

❧ 16 ❧

TUNNEL VISION

Being now in the chemo world, I'm discovering it brooks no competition. It demands my full attention, centre stage. In the past I treated all health problems as events to get over with as soon as possible, and then carry on with the one and only main thrust of my life – the pursuit of happiness and my ministry of spreading the joy of God through the astonishing lens of Incarnation. I remember a few years ago when, the day after one of my hernia operations, I sneaked out of the hospital without full permission, flew to Dublin and took a clapped-out bus to Tipperary, and then to the Glencomeragh Retreat Centre to fulfil a week's engagement I did not wish to cancel. I spoke at that retreat in the only position from which I was able to function: precariously perched, half standing, half sitting, on the edge of a carefully selected bar stool!

But now it's different. That whole ministry is over. No exceptions. There is only the one agenda. And one item on it. The daily attentiveness needed is constant and all-embracing. Each morning there is a list of self-survival information: hospital visits, things to watch out for, telephone numbers to ring, medication and temperatures to be taken, side-effects to be countered. For hardier souls and bodies than mine all of this may be taken in their stride; for me it's a full-time job. Everything else has to be neglected – the normal demands of work and friendship and the commitments of daily life – and then the restless waiting and hoping for good news of some kind re the chemo and the tumour... And all the while knowing that just looking out the kitchen window can sweep my mind with memories, can bring aching flashbacks to my heart.

❧ 17 ❧

SHATTERED BUT STILL
WHOLE

Saki Santorelli tells the story about a disabled artist who was asked
to create the centrepiece for an international art exhibition. All the
submissions were to be the works of 'disabled' artists. The sculptor
had created "a sphere out of stone, perhaps marble or granite. It was
perfect, with an uninterrupted, smoothly polished surface. After the
sphere was completed, the artist smashed it, then put it back together
with bolts, metal fasteners and bonding agents. Now – full of fractures
– it is sitting in the middle of the gallery, in the middle of America,
labelled SHATTERED BUT STILL WHOLE."[16]

A week ago I began Cycle One of chemotherapy, felt the first waves
of nausea and other side-effects. But the tumour was now blocking the
colon, and my tummy was unbearably sore and swollen because I could
not go to the toilet. I took myself off to A&E where I was immediately
prepared for a stoma operation from which I am currently recuperat-
ing before continuing with the interrupted Cycle Two of the treatment.
I'm now finding it impossible to come to terms with the radical and
life-long changes that have just transformed my life. Stoma and chemo
combined are too much for me. So, the 'shattered' bit of the story puts
my present perception quite well; but the 'whole' bit is but a meaningless word. Like 'lost and found'. The 'lost' part is only too true; the
'found' part is but bitter, wishful thinking. My inherent wholeness is
utterly shattered; my hidden self utterly lost.

Everything within me just now rebels against the pretty phrase,
the frilly imagery, the empty, over-worked quotations, the religious
and superficial mantras – all of which I used to copiously dish out

myself. In our evolving, complicated and paradoxical lives, can it be true that the 'shatteredness' and the 'wholeness' co-exist? Do you have any such intimations in the mystery of your own lives? Do you ever bother about such thoughts and questions? Or does everyone have to wait, like me, for the sudden shattering blow before really understanding, utterly vaguely, the life that lies beneath the life we unthinkingly live, the same life that needs our death to set it free? Does a mother know about such paradoxes of death and life? Does nature? *Ask the Beasts,* a wonderful book by Elizabeth Johnson, explores these glimpses of mystery.

Is the question clear? How would the chrysalis-turned-butterfly reply? Ask the post-womb baby? Ask the drop of wine, the crust of bread? Ask the silent heroines and heroes amongst us. The wise ones tell us that absolutely every human creature must travel this strange, repulsive, sublime journey. No one escapes. Is this true? That without intense loss, pain, failure, emptiness and desperation, the true self, the new creation, the inner divinity will never emerge to transform us eternally? Is there an alternative to Jesus' way of the cross? Practically every other page of this book struggles with questions about suffering. What stirs within you when you allow yourself to ponder on these unavoidable realities in your own life? Maybe you are the one, lucky exception?

☙ 18 ❧

AT QUIET MOMENTS

Regardless of everything I believe I still struggle to grasp that there is a way out of my current abyss. My study, prayer and ministry have all been too superficial. Not wrong or misleading, just too shallow and heady. I must go deeper still. I must allow myself to fall even further. Beyond the mind into the recesses of the heart. "The mind is the surface of the heart," wrote Sufi teacher Hazrat Khan, "the heart the depth of the mind." The way up is the way down. Every world religion witnesses to that contradiction. The Christian hero of a beautiful freedom is a bleeding skeleton skewered to a tree. Hasidic wisdom reminds us that "there are temples of gold whose gates open only to tears". We trample through cemeteries to get to the playground of the young. Every localised embodiment of the sublime divine is carved in the cruciform shadow.

All of this we know at some vague level and yet we do not know it at all. Maybe that's as good as it gets. As spiritual writer Richard Rohr insists, only great suffering and great love will open those windows of wonder just a little, to keep us from utter despair, to keep us moving, believing in some horizon, clinging to any straw of hope. Have you, dear reader, travelled yet in that country of your soul? I feel I'm breaking wide open my life and death in a way I never did before. In quiet moments I place my left hand, nearest the heart, over the bag that covers the red and raw stoma and try to channel my love into it. I hold it close, pouring my deepest self into it, seeing this bleeding lump as the sign, shape and substance of divine love incarnate. As Persian mystic Kabir said of his wound, "I'm wrapping it up carefully in my heart-cloth." No sunsets or spring flowers here. The escaping poo, the soiled sheets, the waiting shadow of the relentless chemo and its cruel side-effects. This work, fierce and uncompromising, will, I fear, demand eternal vigilance – a vigilance at the moment totally beyond me.

❧ 19 ❧

REAL PRESENCE

"God in a speck of dust." I meditate on such phrases of Pope Francis. I find them wonderful, liberating, surprising and truly incarnational. It is one of his ways of expressing something of the radical, deepest mystery of Incarnation. There are no exceptions to the absolute meaning of this richest mystery – everything, but everything, is an embodiment of God, an incarnate form and shape of the divine presence, held together by the love-energy we call the Creator. And this incarnate presence is never something added on later. The full essence of God is in the very being of everything created, and is there from the beginning. In fact God's creations are God's own being incarnate, expressed, formed, tangible and visible *as themselves.*

You may wonder why I keep emphasising these truths. It's because we can know these marvellous things at one level, but be unchanged in the very heart of our lives. And notice that even our most revered and trusted spiritual writers do not always seem to 'get' this sublime insight. Not many are comfortable with deep Incarnation. There must be places, people and happenings, they hold, that are somehow apart from God. They pray to bring God *into* such situations and heal them, from outside, miraculously perhaps. Maybe so. The truest teaching of Christianity would indicate otherwise. Difficult as it may be to understand, there are no exceptions. This morning I was trying to meditate on this mystery in my own situation, in my own struggles for the past weeks: trying to pass stools, to avoid the stoma and the curse of the bag at all costs, to gather all the medication possible to lessen the onslaught of the severe doses of chemo. Then the operation and the challenge of coping with the situation, of failing, of seeing it all as a kind of death sentence. Yesterday I received Holy Communion and was meditating on the wonder of the bread and wine becoming flesh of our flesh, blood of our blood. And then poo of our poo. God in a piece of poo. Incarnation is 'visceral', to use a word of Pope Francis, far more so than a perennial visit to a hygienic crib to see an adult-child with a tinsel halo.

20

TO BE OR NOT TO BE

Drained by the intensity of the current, prolonged heat wave (summer 2018), my desire to live at all costs deserts me, and my thoughts begin to wander. The various chemo treatments may take years of a half-life to reveal any results, moving between questionable levels of existence, condemning me to a caricature of the abundant life. Is not this false pursuit of 'life of any kind at any cost' senseless and silly? Each of us must take responsibility for the authorship of our own lives, and stand on the solid ground of our own experience and common sense. (The whole debate about the legalities and human rights around having assistance to die if we wish this to happen, is, I know, waging at the present moment in social media.) But we are here considering only each patient's option for discontinuing chemotherapy.

In *Heal Thyself,* Santorelli writes of the time he and his sister sat at his very ill mother's bed and listened to her hard "razor's-edge" questions to her doctor. "How long will I have with more radiation and chemo? What will the quality of my life be? How long do I have without more radiation and chemo? What will my life be like if I don't have treatment?" After the doctor did his best to answer her questions she sat upright suddenly, looked at all three of them and said, "I don't want any more treatment. I want to live, even for a little while, like a normal human being. To go home, to be with my family and friends, to go out and walk, to enjoy a nice meal, to go to Massachusetts once more."[17] That's when I crumpled and my tears flowed: ". . . to go to Massachusetts once more."

I have reached a point where it seems safe enough to speak intimately about these matters of life and death to certain others – but only with those for whom it is a personal issue. Everyone has opinions when the conversation is in the abstract; a whole new and poignant dimension sets in when it is a current and personal matter. There are so many aspects of life to be taken into account when coming to a decision regarding our own desire to live. Or not. Sometimes these aspects of one's circumstances and life-situations (for example age, family or other dependents, religion, sheer pain) make it easier to move towards a conclusion about dropping chemo (or having assistance to die). Most people want to minimise human suffering. Meaningless suffering is a terrible thing. There is no need to prolong a half-life, many hold, with years of chemo, for no real reason beyond existence. There is no end to people's values and principles regarding this difficult issue. But when people trust you, I find they reveal many surprising (and hidden) insights about the mystery of their life and death. To be or not to be. One thing is sure. Without a hard-won familiarity with surrendering to the inevitable, without trusting blindly, without a habit of letting go, any free decision will be almost impossible to make.

Part Two

❧ 21 ❧

THE ABUNDANT LIFE?

"It hits you so hard. Your body is aching. You can't eat. You can't taste anything. You can't feel anything in the tips of your fingers. You can't go for a walk. You're looking out the window at everyone else playing. You have to dig deep, I mean really deep. I'm not frightened to die but I don't want to die." According to the Sunday Independent this was what Ruth Morrisey said in her court evidence against the Irish Health Service Executive.[18] Ruth has small children, a loving husband, she is young and she is needed. Her death will be because of the incompetence of others. But I have lived my life, my condition is no one's fault. I have no dependents. How different our stories are around the most significant dimensions of a human life.

"The argument in favour of euthanasia can be very compelling in certain circumstances," said Gerry Andrews. "Four years ago I would willingly have accepted such an option, if only it had been available to me. Cancer had taken my beautiful young wife some years previously and now it engulfed my body. Chemotherapy, radiotherapy, dialysis, blood transfusions, endless medical procedures – infections, pain, sickness, exhaustion – can't stand, can't walk, can't sleep, too tired to talk, no energy to read. 'On a scale of one to ten,' a nurse asked, 'how's the pain today?' 'Why stop at ten?' I ask. 'How can I help?' asked a friend. 'Bring me a gun instead of grapes!' came my swift reply. 'Is this a battle worth fighting?' 'Yes! Yes! Yes!' I scream to myself!'"[19]

I marvel at the courage of Ruth and Gerry. I cannot find the same strength within my own soul. It is too soon. Realising that my coping is challenged by the double whammy of colostomy and chemotherapy during the same weeks, I try not to think about the future, but to look forward to the small satisfactions like having rindless marmalade even though it's on white bread, like managing to change my stoma bag without making a mess, like walking for an extra five minutes before getting exhausted, like thinking of the wonder-filled vastness of our universe. There's no point in comparing myself negatively to Ruth or Gerry. All our lives are so different, our ways of receiving sudden bad news, our ways of living with hope, or dying in despair. Above all, I hang on to the belief in 'Something Bigger' that takes care of us, something we are born with, something that loves us, something that is always looking out for us, something that is ready to die for us.

22

NO EGOS ON WARD FOUR

Just three other old men on the ward, unshaven and unshod, a little desperate to survive. We were not too worried about how we appeared, or the niceties of polite company, each of us stuck in the thoughts and anxieties of our own private worlds. No place to hide here. Our peculiarities, ticks and idiosyncrasies were there for all to see. No point in trying to hide our 'imperfect' bodies. If we grow by subtraction then something was definitely happening here! I suppose you could say we had reached a level of basic authenticity, stripped of distinctions and titles, successes or gifts. Our bare selves. One man was struggling, as I was, with the combined shock of a stoma operation and colon cancer. We humbly rang for the night-nurse for help when we made a mess. Is this the promised abundant life? I cynically asked no one in particular. Is this the visceral experience of Incarnation that I had always prayed for? I cynically wondered. Surely not! Surely nothing as raw, crappy and demeaning as this?

Only a few months ago we had waited in the pre-dawn woods of the Ammerdown Retreat Centre for the first stunning glimpse of the Easter Morning sun. And it came. It came and flooded the silent trees and the waiting watchers with a sublime, warm and healing light. More mirage than true experience, I now bitterly reflect. Our transfiguration moment was not a reward; it was preparation. At least for me. How have I lived so long and learnt so little? How have I managed to miss the whole point of Incarnation, to so conveniently ignore the basic Christian symbol of a near-skeletal human being, drained of health and spirit, like myself now, bleeding in despair on a wretched cross? Oh yes, the peace activist Berrigan brothers nailed it all right. "Before you pray to follow Jesus consider how well you look on wood."

✤ 23 ✤

LIVERPOOL RAIN ·

I woke up this morning, not with a new look of wonder in my eyes, about which I have waxed eloquent in the past, as many of you may remember, but with an unwanted bedfellow: the dreaded stoma bag. Already the ward is sticky with this endless heatwave; and is full of nurses and doctors. The pain is intense; the sickness too. Is this a side-effect of the interrupted chemo nausea? Or is it the pain from my new stoma wound? Either way, it suddenly strikes me once more, THIS IS IT! As before, I remember that this is the only way for me to experience intimacy with the love we call God. It is the way of darkness, of the cross, of the death that I unwittingly asked for! It was what I was born for, what comes to everyone, one day or the next, one way or another.

Even after decades of studying, teaching, writing about the way to heaven, I never expected it would suddenly flatten me like this. Never! It is union with God I prayed for but never suspected that the answer would be as terrible as this. Or was it an answer to any-thing? And have I just been a gullible believer in a phantom deity. The desperate, panicky thoughts and fears keep engulfing my soul. To survive the next few weeks, months, years, I must now learn to freely choose, every morning, every hour, every moment of every day, the way of courage. And to hold on to that decision no matter what. There is a whirlpool of spinning night and vanishing dawns in the space of each nanosecond of my life at present.

An hour ago the stoma nurses showed me (again!) how to empty and change the colostomy bag. It's all about liquid poo, passing wind, sickening smells, and the losing battle with hygiene. You cannot imagine a scenario more unsuited to the incarnate presence of God.

Grace does indeed come in many disguises. And yet, for me at least, and just now, that challenge to self-control, dignity and self-esteem seems to be the focus of grace, the murky path of light, the *only current experience of Incarnation*! Is this what Pope Francis means by visceral, by fleshy? How can these cursed visitations of unwelcome sorrow be the sublime blessing of an incarnating God? Is it all one big joke? The Liverpool rain is still falling.

❦ 24 ❦

SLOW DAWN OVER AINTREE

The days move slowly on but there are no changes to each morning's shock. Now I know that my condition is not a nightmare from which I will awaken. The same dull fog envelopes my heart and my mind. I try so hard to make some sense of it all, to find reasons not to despair, to glimpse the tiny light of a vague comfort. With grim humour I remember a story about a believer who maintained that every day he woke up as a convinced atheist. But as the morning wore on, and as he resurrected his favourite understanding about the Faith, by lunchtime he was once more a Christian!

My world revolves around an empty bag. Grace for me lies in whether the blocked poo, in a blocked colon, can find its way along its new pathway, still bleeding, into that waiting stoma bag. Can you believe it? Is the glory of God reduced to this? I recall again Pope Francis spoke of the divine beauty of a speck of dust. Here am I seeing the work of the Holy Spirit in a speck of poo! Please do not be offended at my repetition of this unfamiliar spiritual imagery. It is a small, non-negotiable consequence of the traditional theology of nature and grace. Ours is a bloody, broken, blemished and beloved story of love, suffering and redemption. There is no alternative to these truths. This is the only way for me these days. But it was the same for the crippled, pitiful and destroyed body and mind of a distraught and shrunken Jesus on a tree of torture, and it is the same for everyone in their own particular way of the cross.

And the same for Mary too. While unrecorded in our so-hygienic infancy narratives, Mary, as we have just been remembering, would have gasped and pushed and done all the things that any normal mother giving birth would do. There would have been screaming and blood and water and a placenta on trodden, dirty straw; there would have been a bewildered baby Jesus who would have been gasping for air, learning to breathe, and later, to be potty-trained like any other child. Seems like our Church, in its teaching and preaching, has perennially skipped so many of the early details that would have indicated the true humanity of our Saviour. What was it afraid of?

In my last book *An Astonishing Secret* I tried to explain, in a spiritual way, the interconnection, the interdependence, the utterly mutual identification, for the Christian, of Creation, Evolution and Incarnation – all the work of the divine love-energy called the Holy Spirit. Who would have thought that the actual experience of this sublime revelation, this eternal human design, this deeply spiritual and theological mystery would have become so shockingly clear to me, so radically experienced by me, in the healthy function of the humble bowel, sending some welcome specks of excrement into my waiting bag!

❦ 25 ❦

ONE SEA, MANY RIVERS

Occasionally the despair lessens, the depression lifts, and possibilities emerge. I have always found a healing in understanding something more deeply. During this time in my life only a stark honesty survives. Tortured questions come unbidden: 'Is there a God at all?', 'What do I really believe?', 'Has my life been all on the surface?', 'Why do I now question so many things about Catholic Christianity?', 'How deep does childhood indoctrination go? How long does it last?', 'Are all religions much the same?' Between waves of shadows, this last familiar question returns. Here behind the drawn curtains of my ward cubicle, I can think what I like!

I honestly have no doubt that all the wisdom traditions and religions stream towards the same ocean of love and final unity. I believe that Taoism, Buddhism, Christianity, Judaism, Hinduism and Islam are all equally in their own way, inspired by the One Being, to reveal different aspects of the Holy Mystery. We are not forbidden to see the titles Tao, Mother of Life, Creator, Brahman, Great Spirit, Gracious Mystery, God, Allah, Yahweh, Reality, Being, Infinite Source as beautiful names for the very same Love. Christianity's contribution would centre around the astonishing and unique revelation that we call Incarnation.

Lord Krishna, in his incarnate immanence and transcendence, in his union with humanity and with Brahman, has been called 'The Unknown Christ of Hinduism'. Jewish scholar Rabbi Rami Shapiro believes that each faith is like a language; each reflects on the mystery by way of its own form and colours. To know God better we need to become more multilingual! And you will be astonished at all the detailed similarities of each religion's revelations.

Again, rather than making superhuman efforts to touch Nirvana, to get to heaven after we die, Taoism and Buddhism remind us that everything real, true and loving is already flowing through us right now in what happens each day. All is perfect just as it is! Our calling is to go with this divine/human flow, to be an essential part of it. This understanding of the mystery of life is the same for all true religions. And it lies at the heart of Christianity. (That is the whole point and purpose of the way I now pray.) So much misleading baggage needs to be discarded so as to set our supple and fragile souls free to fly. The real truth of the Christian community of love as revealed in Jesus is groundless and boundless; it is a dynamic healing and liberation, experienced both personally and universally.

In his *Perennial Wisdom for the Spiritually Independent* Shapiro writes that there is but one Reality (of many names) which is the source and substance of all creation. It is the universal and dynamic being of all evolution, and every thing, and each one of us, is an expression and manifestation of that Reality. Instead of seeking to manifest this vision as fully and faithfully as possible, we tend to identify with, and settle for our many culturally-conditioned, flawed, fearful and closed teachings from our childhood.

❧ 26 ❧

ONE BEING, MANY NAMES

I can no longer believe in any kind of external God who will shrink my tumour just because I bombard him with prayers, pilgrimages, sacrifices and repeated religious routines. But I believe more and more in the indwelling Holy Spirit who is the love-energy of whatever I'm called to endure, to suffer, to accept and to be transformed by. As you read these pages of personal meditations you will notice this recurring insight as I try to cope as best I can with my current situation. The key to so much of our dis-ease, our wisest religions insist, is that we want life to be other than the way it is. "Wisdom begins," wrote Jean Vanier, "when we stop wanting to fight the reality of the present as if it should not exist, and start to accept it as it is."[20] As I'm swiftly learning to my cost, the secret of Christianity, too, is to learn how to live as one with the daily unfolding of what happens. No more; no less. Rather than asking for miracles from above, my prayer now must be about how to gladly accept what is happening in the here and now. This insight, in Buddhist teaching too, is one of the Noble Truths about how to lessen our suffering.

As these reflections flow in and out of my consciousness, I can't help wondering how these thoughts affect my current darkness and fear. The nearest I can get to some kind of peace is to continue surrendering whole-heartedly to that all-embracing Reality, that river of love, that God beyond God, that whole divine milieu that holds and caresses everything that lives, everything that grows, everything that keeps happening at every second of evolution: personal and universal.

Richard Rohr reminds us that this kind of total trust is achieved through a moment by moment choice and surrender. This reminder always gives me hope. Total trust takes time. Too often we think that the grace of sacramental vision, of the new way of seeing, of the desired intimacy with God, comes suddenly and then stays with us. In a sense that is true; all we have to do is to become aware of this sublime gift. But awareness takes time. God's incarnate grace is, in a sense, bound by the laws, times and tempo of an evolving and developing Creation.

St Paul mentions the light of God's eyes that we try to reflect each day until, after much practice, we begin to become the light itself. Ours is an Incarnation-inspired spirituality. It has its own timing. We awaken slowly from the sleep of our limited conditioning to know the transforming potential that is latent within us all. A huge problem is that this rude awakening usually comes with an All-Mighty and tragic shock. If this is true, does it make you desire to take your life really seriously before being forced to do so when the bad times come?

❧ 27 ❧

METAPHORS FOR
MEDITATION

Because of the above images and meditations about how God might
be understood, about how the Great Spirit might be experienced even
at a time of no consolation, I'd like to give a few further examples
that might help you, too, in the journey of your soul. I quickly fell out
of love with the 'seminary God' who existed 'out there' somewhere.
The only God I can truly give my all to now, and adore, (and only in
glimpses) is the Lover who lives and loves in the depth of my sinful
heart, and of the heart of all life; who is the dynamic personal and
universal love-energy that drives and draws the world towards its
final goal and fulfilment in the Divine Reality of a transformed Creation. Only images and metaphors this big would enable me to believe
beyond doubt that everything I was suffering, every temptation to
despair that I was enduring, every abject feeling that was sweeping
over me, were all deeply and lovingly inhabited by the same beautiful
and loving Source and Creator.

During midlife, after "entering the dark wood of sin", spiritual
writer Carlo Carretto, an Italian monk who died in 1988, reveals that
he now lived "bathed in God's light, a full searching light which pen-
etrates every corner of my being, and filtered through it like the sun
through the leaves of the forest. I feel immersed in God like a drop
in the ocean, like a star in the immensity of night, like a lark in the
summer sun or a fish in the sea. In God I feel like a child in its mother's lap, and my finite freedom everywhere touches his being which
wraps me round tenderly; my need to grow and evolve and my thirst
for fulfilment are sated every minute by his living presence."[21]

Even though I currently cannot embrace this kind of imagery in its fullness, I love the 'bigness' and extravagance of the sentiments. For Carretto, God's life and love floods us as soon as we are ready to receive it. This readiness, for me at least, and just now, is reached by sieving each second (as you would do with flour) so as to live out its inner meaning, filtering the moments of pain through the prism of Love's 'Now'. I'm trying to only occupy the ever-present moment of what is happening at this instant in my mind, and to my body. This is the only space for God's lovely, weeping face to draw close to mine. At the moment, and to my surprise, I'm discovering that my utter conviction of the unconditional love of God for me and for all Creation, has so little to do with the hellhole I seem to be inhabiting these bleak days.

Yet my only hope is to keep renewing my trust in a divine lover whose incarnate compassion is never far away. Every pulse of the universe, every vibration of energy – all are anxious as a mother to heal her ailing child. Every heartbeat of God, every incarnate grace, every single thing that happens – all are somehow beaming into my body, utterly and lovingly intent on repairing, restoring and resurrecting all that is deficient, incomplete, unaligned to the unfolding of God's plans and out of tune with the hymn of the universe. I need to feel the rhythm of the heart of Mother Universe, Mother Evolution, Mother of Humanity, Mother of all Creation. May God forever deepen in me, clarify for me, the aching glimpses of an impossibly enchanting love.

❧ 28 ❧

BIG PICTURES

In the book already referred to, Shapiro also wrote: "Everything is a facet of the one thing. Think in terms of white light shining through a prism to reveal the full spectrum of colour perceivable by the human eye – red, orange, yellow, green, blue, indigo and violet. Each of these colours is part of the original whole and cannot be separated from it. Turn the light source off and the colours disappear. Now apply this metaphor to the world around you. Everything you see, think, feel, and imagine is part of, and never apart from, the same Source. The list of names for this mysterious Source is long; the reality to which they point is the same."[22]

For the Christian, the Source is God who is both transcendent and immanent, universal and personal. The holy intimacy is in the depths of the human soul, in every cell of our most profound being – and in the cosmic urgency of a billion expanding universes. The ego-self is so cramped; the Christ-self so spacious and expansive. When I am locked up in my own private pain, these glimpses of possibility are redemption indeed.

"Imagine," writes spiritual writer James Finlay, "that you are out walking on the beach and God asks you to pick a grain of sand, any grain."[23] He then tells us that no matter what grain of sand you choose, God's own self is present in it. Furthermore, since the whole universe flows from God and subsists in God, you have in your hand a grain of sand in which you, along with the whole universe, and everyone and everything in it, is wholly present. So, it seems, no matter what you might choose, you realise you are choosing something in which God is wholly present, loving you, and all people and things, into being. As you would expect, my mind jumped to my own condition, and I wondered how God was present in the bleeding stoma that had already changed my world, in the cancer cell that would change it even more.

I'm learning that the journey is inward, and expansive. It is not going to be a fixated obsession with my own misery. Rather the opposite. It is answering a call to take my pain outside myself, into the wider field of Suffering, into the fullest reality of What Is, into the Final Intimacy. Our inner, deepest attitudes and horizons hold the key to our wider awareness, to our expanding consciousness of things. A clerical emphasis on outer behaviour, on obedience to cerebral doctrines has all but destroyed the soul of contemplation, of true spirituality, of tender young children. A friend Kevin sent me an email. "To live in contemplative communion," he wrote, "is to live with the eye of the heart open; to see behind and beneath the veils of limited sense into the mystery of sacramentality, the mystery of divine presence made manifest equally in light and dark. It is the call to recognise in every creature the living breath of the Holy Spirit, to identify God's mysterious, supporting and equal presence in the heat wave and in the stormy thunder. It is the call not to waver in understanding the healing wholeness at the heart of our brokenness, whether of mind, heart, body or soul. When we're out of control, falling fast, we must stretch out for the reaching hand. We do not have to understand or believe that it is there. But it is."

$\sharp$ 29 $\sharp$

BITING THE BULLET

"Your time of trial is truly here," wrote Marion. That brief sentence unlocked something very important for me. 'Why?' you might ask. I do not know! It named, I think, something I needed to recognise. It grounded me in the right place. It focused my bewildered mind on the truth of the moment. To ease my dis-ease a friend, Gabrielle, sent me a quote from Donald Nicholl's lovely book *Holiness*. "The nearer we get to the Holy One the more intense the demands made on us if we are to continue growing. There is a sense of shock when we are struck by the intensity of the demands made upon us at this last stage. Up to now, what we, for our part, have been doing is mainly disciplinary."[24]

Reading this, I took 'disciplinary' to mean the attention I paid to my continual preparation, study, prayer around my talks, travels, retreats, writing, silence, and taking responsibility for my life.

Nicholls continues. "When a person observes these disciplines steadily, year in and year out, he may grow serene and balanced. He may appear to an outsider to be so securely centred that nothing could ever shake him. And then something happens. He is struck by a form of suffering so intense that it shakes the very fibres of his being. To him it feels as though he has no centre left – indeed as though he never had a centre, and all his hard-won balance seems to have been shattered. It is at this stage that the seeker is made to feel a complete beginner once more, and to realise the truth of Thomas Merton's dictum that no one can become whole without being plunged into the mystery of suffering, a mystery that is insoluble by analytical reasoning. If you try to solve this mystery by means solely of your reason, it is as though you have been swept out of your depth into the sea, and are stretching out your legs and kicking with them, trying to a grip with your feet on something firm. You are left with a terrible sense of impotence."[25] Why have those words meant so much to me? What are they saying to you?

❧ 30 ❧

STRANGE BEDFELLOWS

Today, Thursday 9th August, was a tough day. The consultants were clear. The months ahead would be no picnic. The side-effects of the drug Cetuximab would not be hilarious. There would be unsightly rashes and significant diminishments. The chemo treatment would go on for longer than anticipated. Much longer. The stoma bag was rumbling like (to my mind) a machine gun. Was everyone looking at me in the café? Where was the nearest public loo with the special space I needed? And foolishly, I had no handy pocket for the portable forty-eight hour chemo drip bottle that was attached to the PICC line with its protective dressing on my upper arm. A low ebb all round. Then I remembered that Costa's had a well-planned loo for distressed punters like me.

This continued at home. How to have a shower while managing a stoma bag with a chemo bottle, a dressing to be kept dry and vomiting to be ready for? And the night ahead! Imagine all those companions for the long hours – the visits to the bathroom, the careful, anxious turning so as not to disconnect anything. Memories of my spectacular and humiliating 4.00 am failures with these accoutrements in the past. Please forgive me. I will spare you the details. I'm sure you have your own list of troubles without my adding to it. Anyway, I've snipped the M&S £29.50 tag from my new jammies and will hope for the best. A favourite quote of mine regarding faith as 'believing in the dawn while 'tis still midnight' does very little for the mood. Neither does Henri Nouwen help writing, "When my spiritual goal is clear, the life I long for must be reachable right now because God is where I am here and now. We do not have to wait for something that will happen later. It is the active presence at the centre of my living..."[26] Why do these comforting thoughts come to other people? But not to me – and certainly not tonight.

❧ 31 ❧

GRACE NOTES

Even at the most fruitless hours of my efforts to pray, the occasional grace note wriggles free from the cacophony of my days and nights. Like a healing touch it escapes the discordance of the caverns of my mind and sweeps into consciousness shaped as the word YES! It suddenly becomes a non-negotiable decision to go with the positive flow of every possibility. All of this kind of resolution is as old as the hills in the 'care of the mind' manuals, but for me, now, it is laced with urgency and desperation. I know how quickly I can lose the energy to delete everything negative in my mind and especially in my heart. My only hope of surviving this depressing place in which I find myself is to move towards the loving response to everything – gently moving out from all emotional and mental blocking, blindfolding, despair, unrest, fear – the list is endless.

We have been down this road, dear reader, in books and retreats, many times already. What is happening here is that I'm seeing it all, reaching this point, groping for solid ground, because I know that this kind of eternal vigilance is my only hope. Yes, Yes, Yes. I will not be sidetracked into any kind of wavering, doubting, loss of intent, or making of space for the demons to creep back in. Something in me knows that this consistent, determined, focused attitude and readiness will, and must, win out in the end. It is a mindfulness truth; it is a spiritual truth; it is a traditional wisdom.

I touched on this approach in *The Healing Habit* where I wrote, "Your thinking has astonishing powers: to darken your life or to make it radiant. You may not know it, but thinking constantly about something – good or bad – is drawing that situation into your own experience. There is a law that orders every moment. There is an extraordinary spiritual power in your thinking, in the images of your mind. That is how you attract the light or the darkness into your heart. Your thoughts become your reality!"[27] This 'law of attraction' will give you what your thoughts are focusing on. So be careful!

Winston Churchill said that day by day we create our own universe. Your life, your happiness is in your hands. No matter what may have gone before, you can now change every situation in your life. "Whatever you ask for, you are already given it, even before you ask for it," said Jesus (Mk 11: 24). What you think about, pray about, you bring about. Helen Keller, blind and deaf from the age of eighteen months, wrote: "Think powerfully, positively and confidently. Once I knew only darkness and silence – before my heart leaped to the rapture of living. Your life will unfold for you as you expect it to." I believe the Holy Spirit does her personal and cosmic work by convincing us of the already divine power of our minds. Occasionally, when I approach the brink, reflecting on this inner incarnate divine-human power makes such a difference to my resolve and determination.

32

NO TURNING BACK NOW

There is the reaching for a kind of total commitment in the parameters I set myself these days. A complete surrender, as I've mentioned already. It opens the heart and broadens the vision. Otherwise, in our fear, we tend to exclude the rest of the world. The events and emotions of the day acquire a sharper intensity, but the horizon is now bigger, the overall picture fills all else, there is a kind of all-embracing throwing of myself into the evolving, inevitable force-field of intensely moving life. I suppose one could call it, in religious terms, an abandoning of oneself to the will of God. Many decades ago, in the seminary, I was already struggling with that challenge. It looks so very different now! Back then there was a choice; tonight there isn't. This, I feel, without being too dramatic about it, is my last chance to avoid despair. It must be all or nothing. Not one exception to that blanket surrender. From whatever perspective, it is the leap into Love. "Oh sacred human heart of Life, I place all my trust in you."

I look for examples among the heroines and heroes of my life. Teilhard de Chardin wrote, "What I cry out for, like every human being, with my whole life and all my earthly passion, is something very different from an equal to cherish: it is a God to adore. To adore... that means to lose oneself in the unfathomable, to plunge into the inexhaustible, to find peace in the incorruptible, to be absorbed in defined immensity, to offer oneself to the fire and the transparency... and to give of one's deepest to that whose depth has no end.'[28] There is something total, complete, quite intense about these revealing words.

Another way of putting this is to see Love itself as the very heart and soul, in the breath and body, the substance and presence, the reality and truth of *everything*. Then, and only then, are we lost in Love.

Then, and only then, are we *becoming* Love. You may not be surprised that a poem we have often shared comes into my mind during meditations such as this one – maybe it's a fitting way to end this reflection. It is called *The Guest House* by the Persian poet Rumi:

This being human is a guest house.
Every morning a new arrival,
A joy, a depression, a meanness,
some momentary awareness comes as an unexpected visitor.
Welcome and entertain them all!
Even if they're a crowd of sorrows,
who violently sweep your house empty of its furniture,
still, greet each guest honourably.
He may be clearing you out for some new delight.
The dark thought, the shame, the malice,
meet them at the door laughing,
and invite them in.
Be grateful for whoever comes,
because each has been sent
as a guide from beyond.[29]

33

PRACTISING DYING

While there is no immediate reason for me to think that I'm on my last legs, the thought these days is never far away. I feel at least, that I'm on a dry run. As Fr Ed Hayes, author of *Prayers for a Planetary Pilgrim*, remarked on one occasion, "I'm practising dying." (This of course, can also mean, 'I'm practising living.') When we ask to become whole and holy, to be saved, we think we are hearing God's response to us in terms of improving our lives, but along the familiar lines of our life's choices: being kinder, becoming more aware of our suffering neighbours, going to confession, defending the Faith (and the Pope!). Especially during Lent and in times of need. Nothing wrong with any of that. But the temptation is always to interpret the message according to our own image and likeness, to reshape our enhanced spirituality along the lines of our usual superficial well-meaning routines. And this too may well be what God wants of us.

Yet the answer to our prayers may be a "demand this night for thy soul" (Lk 12: 20), a shocking ultimate and life-transforming intrusion that seems like the end of everything. What is frightening and unknown will purify and stretch the soul in ways that the familiar just cannot do. For only when we are stripped of all the secure landmarks by the arrival of the totally unexpected can the real and fearful dying eat into us. This (and maybe only this) is what opens us up more fully and more humbly to the unfathomable and ineffable mystery of the heart of God, and at the same time, prevents us from falling back on the old, dry and often mindless routines of the past. Such fierce experiences as mine blast away at the rock-face of our own precious ideas. St John of the Cross reminds us that we learn to understand more by not understanding anything, that we travel more safely when we have no map!

And even then, as I know to my cost and current experience, when our familiar way of living is disrupted or challenged by a new bombshell falling into our lives - either to do with a great loss, a great love or a great suffering - we are still unlikely to let go of our past holy habits, our past devotional certainties, our inherent self-protection from pain, because the dark unknown, the surrender of control, are just too fearful and fearsome. In all of this, as far as I can now gather, the search is not for a new self, but the true self we have always been; not for a new and special name, but reclaiming and recovering the name we always had. And that name is *Beloved*.

❧ 34 ❧

PERSONAL SALVATION?

Many of us valued our personal relationship with Jesus. We would earn our individual salvation, deserve it, and end up in heaven. This will not work anymore; in fact, writes Richard Rohr, it never did. If we profess Jesus as the saviour of the world, he holds, we must not or cannot continue to think of salvation as merely a private matter. Do you? Do I? We are wasting our time trying to be holy alone without turning outwards - forgiving our 'enemy', keeping an eye on the sick neighbour, taking responsibility for the health of our planet. Not to do this, according to Pope Francis in his *Laudato Si'*, is a sin. It also involves challenging, as mercifully as possible, the Church and the Vatican in particular, and speaking up in the face of all corporate, collective and fully institutionalised injustice and even evil. If we think we can say our private prayers, Richard Rohr continually reminds us, and still genuflect before the self-perpetuating, unjust systems of this world, this culture, this religion, our conversion will not go very deep or contribute to the unfolding of history.

This is why contemplation is so utterly central and necessary. There is no one more radical than a real person of prayer because they are not beholden to any religious control or economic system. Truly transformed people organically change the world, while fundamentally unchanged Christians can only conform to the current religious and political systems and collude with them. All of this, in the current state of religious and economic affairs is only too obvious. "Culture will win out every time over the Gospel if it is not critiqued by the Gospel."[30]

Why am I getting a bit preachy here? Wagging the finger again? Well it's because in my own restless reveries these nights and days, the point that gets more obvious to me is the intrinsic link between our inner and outer lives: our personal spirituality and our involvement in the corporal works of mercy; our intimate relationship with the incarnate Holy Spirit and the energy of that relationship in the establishing of some kind of lasting peace – in a micro and macro focus on community reconciliation and the renewal of the world.

As I am experiencing these times of my own anxious confusion and searching for the truth of holiness, there are glimpses of creation's purpose even amid the world's present pain, brokenness and despair. These glimpses recognise the inevitable journey of inward and outward transformation: the simultaneous, continuing transformation of the inward hearts of people liberated by God's astonishing grace through suffering, and the outward transformation of social and economic structures in the light of God's justice.

The resolve and motivation to establish justice and peace can only be born in the individual spiritual journey of the heart. This is not the privatised expression of belief or practice of the external routines that keeps faith in Jesus contained in an individualised bubble and protects us from 'the world'. Rather it is a spiritual journey which connects us intrinsically to the presence of God whose love yearns to save and transform the world. But the first call, arising from the unconditional compassion of our Saviour, is the call to each of us to be the embodiment of God's love in the world. And how, in my new despair, do I begin to be that? And is there still time?

❧ 35 ❧

REASONS FOR HANGING IN THERE

Well, what's the alternative? To whom should I go? Where do the answers lie? Wounded now as I undoubtedly am, there is only one way out – or rather one way in – that of trusting inwardly in blind faith that I, and the world, and all creation are still utterly loved by a God whose name is Love. My bigger, deeper, wider meditative prayer tries to recover my belief that we are eternally connected to the source of life in such a way that nothing, absolutely nothing, can ever sever it – not bad health or imminent death, not betrayal by someone, indeed not even our own destructive acts and sins. Nothing can change God's unconditional love for us. Without some light from that polar star, our hearts will give up. This is the time to dig deeper. Remember our discussion about the inner star that each of us carries, that spark that sometimes springs to life, the *cantus firmus* set deeply into our hearts. That light *never* goes out.

Sometimes dogged, sometimes soaring, there is this one thing, in all that is happening to me, that I've never, ever doubted: that eternal love in every cell of my body. Some people, in the light of my past insistence about God's unconditional love, no matter what, have asked me questions. Now that the visceral awareness of incarnate divine love, the sense of its protection and motherly care is absent from my life, do I still believe in that enduring affection? And was I being presumptuous in my claims about God's unconditional love no matter what? And naïve in connecting it so intimately with memories of my mother's still remembered love? By some miracle of nature and grace, by one burning brand of Incarnational conviction scored into my heart from the beginning, my deepest and abiding belief has held firm even in the storms of these days and nights. Maybe this is the meaning of 'faith'. I believe, my God, help my unbelief.

❦ 36 ❦

WHO AM I NOW?

As many of you may know, I have always wanted to be authentic (and, as you will also know, mostly failed in the effort). As never before, the sheer and searing truth of my current condition will settle for nothing less than utter honesty. The tricks of the mind, the persuasions of the ego, the false practices of decades, the whispers of our own personal prince of lies, will not easily surrender their subtle and invisible power. The huge fear is about what is left of us when all we once regarded as our gifts and graces, our successes and talents, are scattered like chaff on the cutting-floors of our minds. In times of desperation such as I'm now encountering, I realise how riddled with base motives are my most externally religious moments and spiritual exercises. Pope Francis so often refers to the idols of his heart, the hidden temptations that are invisible even to himself! Do you ever devote any time each day to reflect on these matters? Do you think it is an important thing to do? Pope Francis certainly does.

Accepting my physical cancer of the colon is accepting the invisible cancer of my soul. Accepting the poisoning tumour in my bowels is accepting what I'm hiding all my life. Are these statements true? Really true? Is that how it works? How else would I ever know about the presence of the unwanted squatters in my heart, the uninvited guests of my shadow, the ones that it took a terrible tumour to reveal? The legendary hero has to kiss the horrific crone at the well to reveal both his and her beauty. The wound is inner before it is outer, spiritual before physical. Is it worth finding the quiet time each day to reflect on these questions, on your unknown depth, your silent music, your unlived life?

"The work of re-owning your own shadow is essential," writes author Santorelli. "Without undergoing this labour we remain blind, unconsciously driven by those unattended-to forces within us. For all of us, this work is not pleasant. Here we are faced with the enormity of our greed, deception, ignorance, shame, grief and humiliation. Looking into the mirror, we see, without filter, our capacity for self-betrayal, self-deception and false shadows. And so we begin to fall..."[31] I'm well into the falling game just now in my shattered identity. What about you? I dare to ask. Have you experienced a life-changing fall? Sometimes a harsh and decisive fall occurs, maybe through unexpected illness, a divorce, the death of a soul friend or losing a job without any warning. And, in so far as you brought God into it at all, did that experience draw you any closer to God and to yourself or drive you further away?

"In the deserts of the heart, let the healing fountain start," wrote W.H. Auden. Santorelli believes that we cannot escape such an experience in the span of our lives, that we certainly cannot become a person of depth or wisdom without a searing shock, a stripping humiliation, a death of all that is false in us. Is it possible to be ready for this happening? Or is its suddenness the shocking part? Is the cross different for everyone? And are some people more ready for the inner healing, more sensitive to grace, more blessed in their receptive hearts and minds to God's will? Or do we all battle with the demons of weakness, of fragile faith, of shallow and pathetic resolve?

Thomas Merton believed that his fans would be shocked if they could see the litter-strewn streets of his splintered mind. He battled with his demons, his masks, his lies, his temptations. As did Jesus. The only journey worth taking is the one towards inner authenticity, brave honesty and utter integrity. And on arrival, God is found too. It is a moment of the fullest self-discovery, the moment we were created for.

One of the most popular poems in recent years is *Love after Love* by Derek Walcott. You will realise its truth by what it does to your heart.

The time will come, when, with elation,
you will greet yourself arriving at your own door,
in your own mirror, and each will smile
at the other's welcome,
and say, sit here. Eat.
You will love again the stranger who was your self.
Give wine. Give bread. Give back your heart
to itself, to the stranger who has loved you
all your life, whom you ignored
for another, who knows you by heart.
Take down the love letters from the bookshelf,
the photographs, the desperate notes,
peel you own image from the mirror.
Sit. Feast on your life.[32]

When that day comes will you, will I be able to say, with the mystic Merton, when surrounded by the demons that live near cancer, or the next unsuspected tragedy, "At every moment of my life I am exactly where I am supposed to be. And nothing in my life ever goes wrong. Everything is adorable?" Takes some working out, doesn't it?

✦ 37 ✦

THE BURIED LIFE

For mental relief these nights I try to distract myself from the relentless inner addiction to negative thinking with a forced interest in books, in passing news, TV sports and documentaries. Today begins the week of Pope Francis' visit to Ireland for the World Meeting of Families event. The papers are full of the most shocking revelations about the state of the Catholic Church and its leadership, its terrible sins of child abuse and cover-ups, the poisoned inner heart of the Vatican organisation.

Having lived through the troubled decades since the Second Vatican Council, I'm still in utter disbelief about the destruction of the faith by the Roman system. No longer is it a question of the behaviour of some seriously damaged leaders, but of the rotten heart of the Vatican itself. These are serious comments. But many of us have been saying them for decades. And they have been ignored for decades. And still are. There is an evil spirit afoot in the most sacred places and in our hierarchical leadership.

And I completely belong to the clerical mentality at the core of it all. Like a perfect prison, like a terrible unending web, it is impossible to escape from it. We were seduced into it; we fell for the false promises; then it was too late to turn back. There is no one to blame but our own naivety and ignorance and simplistic trust. And of course, a great fear. The terrible revelations in this weekend's social media can be traced back, in large part, to the Institution's insistence on compulsory celibacy – and ordination for males only. This unnatural, un-incarnational and mandatory condition for becoming a loving servant of God's people is at the root of most of the current tragedies raging in the heart of Christ's community.

Three days ago Pope Francis, on the eve of his Irish visit, wrote an abject apology to the world's Catholics, taking responsibility for the Church's failure to take care of her children, for the destruction of innocence, for the evil to which it has turned a blind eye. Today, 21st August, Richard Rohr wrote about the Church's immature teaching in regard to sexuality in general, male power issues in particular, and the enforced undertaking of celibacy which will predictably produce this disastrous result. "Until the Catholic Church disconnects celibacy from ministry, I think we will continue to have ordained men... who are a scandal to the Body of Christ."

And here I am now, at a low ebb, wondering how in God's name literally, I got into this terrible mess. What kind of 'vocation' did I have? What did I understand of compulsory celibacy aged seventeen years in rural Ireland in the fifties? Why is it only now that I think so sadly about those missing teenage years, those decades of a lost life? Was it all a terrible mistake? Is it my current and serious health issues that draw this melancholy around me? I have, of course, as you know, spoken and written about – and suffered for it – these transparently unjust and inhuman Roman Catholic practices. Many of my colleagues do not agree with me; they agree with the system, quite happy with the way things are, fulfilled in their calling. I wonder how they feel during this crucial week as the Church, like never before perhaps, fights for survival. I reflect on these thoughts, and write them down, without any bitterness, but with lots of deepest bewilderment and shafts of anger too. So many buried lives.

> *But often, in the world's most crowded streets,*
> *But often in the din of strife,*
> *There rises an unspeakable desire*
> *After the knowledge of our buried life;*
> *A thirst to spend our fire and restless force*
> *In tracking out our true original course . . .*
> *And long we try in vain to speak and act*
> *Our hidden self, and what we say and do*
> *Is eloquent, is well – but 'tis not true!...*[33]

✤ 38 ✤

ARE WE THERE YET?

It does not take much to shake our faith, to expose the flimsy basis of it, to tempt us to doubt everything. At least, for me, and just now, that is so. The 3.00am questions are relentless. Is there an end to this season of discontent? How many more trapdoors will open at my feet? When does the falling stop? Does the cave-journey twist and turn forever in the darkness? When do I arrive somewhere? When is the journey over? Does the search for ultimate unity go on into infinity? Is it ever possible to live only for the love of God, to do everything simply because it is the way of love?

Why am I surprised at the sudden appearance in my life of a God whose presence to me now is all about endings, confusion, despair and death? Is that not the defined, the main and enduring Christian image of the human God: a failure, a criminal on a bloody cross, despised, tortured, young, ridiculed, a failed Messiah? The whole world knows this. The Christian cross is everywhere. How did I miss it? Why am I so surprised, so shocked when it comes to taunt me now? Have I not read the Gospels? Has not my whole life been spent in pursuing the Incarnation Story in one way or another? Like the misfortunate and unsuspecting man who had built his beautiful barns. (Lk 12: 16-21)

Today my 'quiet' time has a very different feel to it. I must try to come to terms with a God whose face is unfamiliar, whose presence is a kind of absence. I search for hints and sightings, a new clue, a place to wait for her. I do not doubt the divine presence; I just have no sense of it today. Every morning is another descent into the underground caverns in search of the new faces of Love. Its presence is secure, undoubted; its face, however, is covered. Every shape and image of it withdraws into a finer, more elusive one. I repeat, there is never a doubt about its presence – only an impatience for its embrace. It has little to do with intellectual conviction or argument – only with visceral emotion and love-energy. Not a dutiful, soulless belief anymore; it's more about the taste of Sunday's holy bread between my teeth, the felt embrace of a friend's divine blessing, the sensual comfort of exchanging a few words of love and truth. And a cuppa and chat afterwards.

When wrestling with the 'God questions' in the seminary, I remember thinking that whatever evidence there may be of a cruel and vindictive deity, I could never doubt my conviction of divine love. For instance, whatever terrible secrets may be discovered about my mother, I used to argue, nothing would convince me that she did not love me with an astonishing love. That fact, about my mother and God, (indistinguishably interrelated), were simply 'givens', beyond debate, never threatened. My present journey is about exploring the dark interior of the Mystery of Life, of Love, of Being, knowing that I will never see any of it these days except in the darkest and most unexpected outlines.

39

SECOND LOVE

Whether called the 'sacramental vision' or the 'Catholic imagination', that belief in and experience of the beauty beneath the surface of everything, will be forever the unshakeable and astonishing secret of my life. I only hope I have many more years to play with this incarnate heart of God in the most sublime music, in the most forlorn fallen leaf. What is happening is that I must expand that reality, reflection, incarnation and presence of the Christian God into the shape of my current darkness, my deepest loss, my upended life, my bracketed beautiful certainties and convictions. Love, because of its infinite depth and height, its mysterious forms and faces, will always be beyond the reach of my imagination, and greets me now as the face of death, of loss, of a shocking emptiness. "To come to the knowledge that you have not," wrote St John of the Cross, "you must come by the way you know not". So, love and faith and courage. I'm all determined this morning to climb this other mountain, to sink to these other depths, and to always feel a beckoning, an irresistible and effortless allurement into something greater, something more interior, something more pure, something more invincible – an utterly compelling love.

Think of someone you truly love. Life is then a journey into the endless mystery of that love. Any surprises, changes, even shocking new awareness about the loved one, will not change that basic foundation. All the poets and saints have written so well about that. The lover stays open, becomes aware of the invincibility of true love, may well have to keep adjusting, dying to previous certainties, but still believing in the enduring presence of that unshakeable love. My present thoughts and energy are running along these lines. There is a Love that can only be approached through darkness and death, so great and deep is its mystery. I can feel a strange welcome from behind the locked doors of my stalled mind, through the death that spells not an end to the once intense love, but a keener desire to find its beating heart even more intensely in my wilder abandon to the Mystery.

And I do believe that far from having to jettison any of the cherished images and experiences of God's astonishing and unconditional love and incarnate presence in our lives and our world, it is those very heartfelt convictions and delightful 'human' experiences that have prepared my soul to understand Incarnation; recognising in an ever-clearer, ever more intense, ever more intimate way how God's love is incarnate *in and as* those very experiences. We love each other with the same love that God loves us. That is why human is so beautiful. It is God's only way of holding us close. With great tenderness R.S. Thomas wrote *A Marriage*:

> *We met under a shower of bird-notes.*
> *Fifty years passed, love's moment*
> *in a world in servitude to time.*
> *She was young; I kissed with my eyes closed and opened*
> *them on her wrinkles.*
> *'Come' said death, choosing her as his partner for*
> *the last dance. And she, who in life had done everything*
> *with a bird's grace, opened her bill now*
> *for the shedding of one sigh no*
> *heavier than a feather.*[34]

✣ 40 ✣

IS THIS THE 'REALLY REAL'?

Other meditation images come and go this morning. In response to my friends Martin and Maria's loving invitation to reflect on my challenged convictions and certainties now, I wrote these paragraphs. Contemplation is like searching for precious diamonds hidden in the coal-black night of the mines, not in the clear bright daylight of the usual incarnate maps and images of nature's beauty, but in the death at the heart of all Creation. Even in my current shock and confusion around the sudden shattering of my cancer-hit life, everything I have ever believed about God, everything I've ever written about divine love, beauty and compassion incarnate in everything and everyone, is, in no way doubted, revised or questioned – not a comma, not one word. It is all now a continuing journey of the soul, a further introduction to the meaning of love, another image, truth of the incomprehensible mystery that our normal religious practices, beliefs and dogmas don't even scratch.

All my spiritual, mental and emotional nourishment now arises from a wholly changed and purified understanding of the world I live in, the life I live, the power of my imagination, the beauty of God, the meaning of an evolving incarnation. The credos and catechisms of my life's religion offer scant spiritual nutrition. In fact, just now I find them mostly irrelevant. They actually distract from the world of intimacy; they distort the clear call to a felt and true love. My whole intense heart-focus and searching are now happening in a deeper milieu.

A new understanding is being born of a non-dual and eternal connection, of the one-ness of being, of the truth of the imagination, of the practical, mystical, physical echoes of the soul, of the indwelling

Blessed Trinity, of the Incarnation of the Holy Spirit, of the heaven in every breath, of the God in a heartbeat, and of the felt pulse of the dark demon of death. The outer routines of religion have, of course, their essential place, but just now, and for me, my thoughts and feelings are about relationships with God, with the world, with community, with myself.

In the face of these truths, any personal failures of faith, any passing doubts about the mystery, any cerebral arguments about contradictions and confusions (utterly important as these may be in their native context) have little relevance to my story now. This, for me, is not the time for discursive distinctions and comparisons but for the connections of love, and the experience of an intimacy that precedes knowledge. American modernist poet Wallace Stevens wrote:

> We come
> To knowledge when we come to life.
> Yet always there is another life,
> A life beyond this present knowing,
> A life lighter than this present splendour . . .
> Not an attainment of the will
> But something illogically received,
> A divinisation, a letting down
> From loftiness, misgivings dazzlingly
> Resolved in dazzling discovery.[35]

Part Three

❧ 41 ❧

THE CUT-OFF LIFE (1)

As mentioned in the introduction to this book, I have tried to be faithful to my thoughts, doubts and temptations, recounting them as they happened without adding any explanations or spiritual make-over. I'm also trying, as the days and weeks are passing, to reflect on the whole happening in the light of the Incarnation. Everything expressed is entirely my own story. I already know that many, including priests, will struggle with the themes and heart of my story. And that, of course, is just as it should be. Knowing that you will read these glimpses into my troubled soul without censoring or judging or criticising them, but receiving them in your open heart, is, I'm sure, contributing to my healing and strengthening. Thank you.

What do I mean by 'the cut-off life'? I wasn't long ordained when one day it dawned on me that priesthood and its accoutrements – clerical attitudes, clerical dress, clerical assumptions, clerical lifestyle – had, at a stroke, distanced me from the normal way that people relate, communicate and form community. In both France and Ireland, even at that time, we have been called 'the hard men'. Today, this very week, in the light of the scandals and cover-ups of shame across the whole world, the names they call us are both justified and terrible.

Before the recent, numbing scandal revelations, in the heydays of priesthood, we needed little convincing, triumphant as we were, committed celibates, that we had the inner track on God's secrets. As priests we were told, and we believed it, that we were detached from the world, that we no longer belonged to it; we were *in it but not of it*! Our church-going, our home-training, our local liturgy, our schooling, our seminary training, tainted disastrously by a deeply flawed theology, were all unavoidably and not intentionally of course, basically anti-Incarnation, anti-Creation, anti-human. However, there is no need to go over that old ground again. I only mention it because it has all come back to me in recent twilight reveries. Forgive me for this, but, you see, it is the album of my life, the very heart of my formation as a human being. These are the experiences that flood back, now that I've had to stop working and face the blank page of my future.

42

THE CUT-OFF LIFE (2)

Compulsory celibacy is a kind of sin, an assault against God's will and nature. At last it is now being recognised as such, especially since Pope Francis began pointing to clericalism, its sister, as the major underlying threat and destroyer of the true Church. Let me avoid the minefield that this could drag us into! Here I'm just pointing out that one of the fallouts of the mandatory celibacy and clericalism of the priest's life is the unavoidable reality of being cut off from normal society. Again, I can hear the voices calling me a traitor to the cause, disloyal, twisting the truth to suit my opinions. But please remember, I'm only recalling the memories, convictions and awakenings that are filling my soul during these ever-so-strange days and nights. It is so interesting what flows back into our hearts and minds when the chips are down and the hours are long and empty. Maybe these are, and always have been, the real and hidden issues in a priest's life.

Having no partner, no children, no networking with other families, at so many levels, cuts us off from most normal and meaningful interactions, connections and shared experiences with others. Our lives can often become something we do, get through, rather than deeply live. These are sad things to say. And there are a very great number of exceptions. I'm simply repeating my thoughts at a low time. I'm also convinced of the truth of most of them. Consider, for instance, the unbelievable assumption that this most unjust, exclusive and unchristian way of selecting male priests was God's will, with no real evidence from the Gospels or tradition for that certainty. Yet the conservative certainties of our leaders will have no truck with these comments of mine. (Notice the hierarchy's attitude to former president Mary McAleese's presentations critiquing the Church during the current visit of Pope Francis to Ireland, August 2018).

Of course there are so many happy priests. And they would condemn me to high heaven for these things I'm saying. But during the many priests' retreats I've given in my life, I've heard a different story, the true story of the terrible destruction of human beings, of the priest's own humanity and far too many other lives caught up in the sometimes impossible mess of human needs and authoritarian attitudes. Some priests managed to hang on to their true essence, their authentic, essential selves; many of us did not. The enemy, we were warned, back in the fifties, was a failure in prayer. Falling in love was the cancer; suppression, sublimation and confession were the cure. Emotion was the threat; detachment was the safeguard; becoming too human was the risk; the carapace of clericalism was the precaution. Clericalism is a collective malaise which keeps the vibrant, abundant life at bay. It quarantines us for life from the personal and communal expression of relationships, emotions and the lovely grace of the tenderness which Pope Francis is trying to restore to the hearts of all God's people: all who are trying to be more like the One most beautiful, divine and human heart that ever lived.

In *The Last Dreamers* priest-poet Padraig Daly, during the end of last century, wrote with compassion about an approaching winter for priests and for the Church:

> We began in bright certainty,
> Your will was a master plan
> Lying open before us. Sunlight blessed us,
> Fields of birds sang for us,
> Rainfall was your kindness tangible.
> But our dream was flawed;
> And we hold it now,
> Not in ecstasy but in dogged loyalty,
> Waving our tattered flags after the war
> Helping the wounded across the desert.[36]

Referring to humanity in general, Saki Santorelli writes, "Much of the time we live as if shrouded by a thin veil, an internal frost, a coolness that moves out through the skin, rising up between ourselves and the world, leaving us feeling grey, lifeless and enclosed... We are trained *into* it in a thousand ways because it appears to make life easier. More tolerable. Secure."[37] The metaphor I used in those first years of cycling through the streets of my first parish, doing house-to-house visitation, was of looking at people, their families and ordinary lives as though distanced from them by invisible glass. We were the men in black. The mysterious men who were different. We alone could change the bread; we alone could forgive the sins.

The reader may sense loss and regret in these musings. Yes and no. Certainly not a hint of bitterness but only a kind of joy that I have the courage, the freedom, the chance to reveal my inmost feelings and, I have no doubt, the feelings of millions. There were wonderful days and happy relationships. We felt called and privileged. Many ambitious ones were promoted for their devotion to duty. These were great decades for the Church triumphant. In general priests were happy. We were married to the Church; the parish was our family. But that flawed promise soon lost its lustre. They were actually the decades when child abuse was most rampant.

Please remember that I'm telling bits of my story now as my current trials are affecting my deeper understanding of things. Many of the above reflections on the sin of clericalism and of mandatory celibacy have arisen from the night when I was thinking about the people that have changed my life, those who somehow left the imprint of their hearts and friendship in my very being. Among those were the faces of those I have hurt, and to whom I never had the chance to say I'm sorry. I'm truly saying it now.

✦ 43 ✦

AND IT'S STILL ONLY
AUGUST!

It's still only August. It feels like a lifetime since June. With the emerging weekly details gleaned from conversations with the cancer consultants, the picture just gets darker. I try not to exaggerate or panic or get too depressed. I've been wondering just how much bad news one can take within a few weeks. (I'm always aware of the infinitely greater pain of those we read about every day, but my own suffering continues at times to block out the universal realities.) Is there an infinite capacity within the human spirit, within our deepest natural and graced capacities to cope, to endure, to suffer and eventually to find some stirring of new life? Is there a sacred space in us that can one day, or night, be found, where something invincible reaches a balance, a fragile tipping-place where the scales tip on the right side? And how long can I wait for this to happen?

A core belief, variously expressed in most of the great faiths, is about the ever-present, the indestructible true self, the ever-incarnate breath of God. Thomas Merton describes this soul as "that virginal spot, the beauty of people's hearts where neither sin nor desire can reach, the core of their reality, the person that each one is in God's eyes. If we could all see ourselves in this way…" Reflecting on these words in my frail times, brings me some comfort. They help to protect the torn fabric of my mind from further damage. But the challenge is that these realisations are useless until they are painfully and slowly incarnated into the essence of our presence with everyone we encounter, until there is a deep awareness of Merton's observation at every step of each day.

I gain confidence from the loving wishes of my friends for me just now. I just know that the love in their hearts needs no constant external expression, but works its way across the expanses of our world. They are the most incarnate forms of God's healing grace. Without it, all the Masses and rituals in the world will be empty shells. And as is too often the case, utterly meaningless. Theologian Karl Rahner even described these outer and shallow repetitions of what we believe to be at the heart of the Catholic faith as 'worthless'.

44

YOU'RE MAKING A FUSS ABOUT YOURSELF!

Another worry I carry these times is whether I'm making a mountain out of a molehill, whether readers or friends will wonder why I seem to be making such a fuss about these matters. 'Does he really know what others go through? Does he think about young parents with severe illnesses, with children to rear, parental love constantly to provide, finances too, and a hundred other necessities which they are daily required to fulfil?' Believe me I do. I try to. And I agree entirely with such judgements. And if these pages never see the light of day that will be the only reason.

At the moment I do hope that apart from helping me to get through this desert time, some of you may find some meaning in this un-corrected, un-tampered-with flow of rather miserable thoughts and feelings. And I truly hope that you will notice the wee flickers of light that keep slipping in. But human as we are, any intimations of resurrection must take time. The truth of my situation has no room for pretend cures or rewards or (expected) miraculous answers to prayers. Remember the long-lasting darkness that almost invariably (and necessarily) descends even on the souls of great women and men, great souls like those of Jesus and Mary. Incarnation is not about 'the quick fix'; it is woven into time and space.

And then silently, among those strange and threatening visitors mentioned by the poet Rumi in his *The Guest House* (see no 32 'No Turning Back'), another whisper from a stranger slips into and nestles, with a sure sigh, in the waiting, lonely place. A special friend Annie sent me this:

Today will be the black night
and pain will spear each pulse –
I know it;
the dark tunnel on and on –
this I understand;
life that is as death for you –
I feel it.
I know, understand, feel,
Because it was for me
A like stretch of time;
by this I am marked
so that now with utter sureness
I can urge you, beloved human,
to search out your courage;
even if the bitter stone
in your chest is, you think,
for ever,
and you can take no more, hold fast, hold fast;
that stone will melt,
the tunnel will become
a flow of discovery
and it will be again morning –
I have seen it.[38]

❧ 45 ❧

AND THERE'S MORE!

Each time that I fear I may be overreacting to my increasingly shattering news, and hoping it cannot now get any worse, *wham!* another shot across the bows. Just when I begin to find a firmer foothold for my next few hours of thinking, my brain is scrambled once again. The consultant speaks of another clarification of the severity of the side-effects of the new drug, another realistic assessment of the effectiveness of the chemo in the light of the latest biopsies taken, and there is another decision to make regarding continuing with the stoma challenges and the chemotherapy at the same time. Every time I let go of my tight grip on my mind it races towards the precipice of grief; every time I slip outside the safe boundaries of the here and now, a sheer panic violently twists the normal patterns of mature thinking. No escape today. No silver lining. No resurrection from my personal tomb.

Once again I turn, in need, to my copy of *The Healing Habit* for help. "Be prepared for a struggle, a kind of battle – even a kind of dying – along the path of this journey to healing, health and wholeness that you have chosen. This is the guidance of all our wisdom traditions, our enlightened ancestors, our religious elders. But they also encourage you not to be afraid of the inner conflict, those dark forces, those subtle demons of despair. In fact, in a most mysterious paradox, those teachers all agree that it is often only at the point of that persuasive temptation to quit that the real dawn of a new perspective, a new way of seeing and being, can emerge in the here and now. Pain, somehow, is the teacher within; suffering, the hidden gift."[39] You prayed for the grace to purify your ego, your vanity, your inauthenticity, your conceit. Now your prayer is being answered! This is the way. And there is no other.

Even though I believe them with all my heart, I find little comfort, this evening, in those fine words. How I wish I could practise them, to get over the fear, to look with acceptance at the worst possible scenario; to imagine being free of those hurting anxieties that surround me just now – and maybe, in the same grace-process, liberate myself from many other deeper-seated shadows. Just glimpses would be enough for a start. For instance, what if I could face up to the side-effects one by one? When my hair begins to fall out: to shave it all off! It would be a new adventure. When the rash covers my body and inflames my face: to go shopping as usual and talk to those I meet without too much embarrassment. When my stoma bag gurgles and splutters like rain going down a drain, or it needs to be emptied or changed when I'm sharing a coffee and chat with someone: to smile calmly and explain the situation. And then the more serious ones.

I already know my normal life is over and my work projects are all cancelled forever. Absorbing ambiguous drugs could continue for the rest of my life. I see myself as a skeletal invalid wasting away behind lace curtains, looking at real life happening, as usual, outside the window. I know that all of this is a bit dramatic, and panicky, but in the middle of the night that's how it goes. Remember I'm writing what is happening in my deepest heart, far removed from any contrived happy ending. I wonder if Jesus on the cross knew somehow that it would all turn out fine and dandy at the end? I very much hope not. Otherwise I'm finished!

46

UNDERSTANDING IS
HEALING

Healing comes in many ways: medication, conversation, music, the senses, nature, various vibrations... At night, when things get ominous in my head, I'm discovering that one dimension of meditation brings a temporary calm and comfort: when the mystery of life and love, the meaning of God's Incarnation, in its graciousness surrenders itself temporarily to my desire to understand more fully. So many of you will have travelled with me in my perennial and daily efforts to grasp, to 'get', to understand something of the love and meaning at the heart of everything. Most of our time together has been spent in pursuit of those first graces of the Holy Spirit – wisdom, understanding, deep knowing. And now and then, like stray blossoms in winter, like faint grace notes in the storm, like a hint of unexpected perfume, something sings in our minds, and our relentless search to know more about the astonishing mystery called God is momentarily satisfied.

Is there a better way of saying these things? I suppose we are made to know and to be known, to open our hearts to the power of that deep need to search for, to become one with, to become part of. The moment of grace can often come suddenly in the dead of night while my conscious mind is otherwise engaged, battling the dark in another place. Usually, as you might expect, it has something to do with experiencing the closeness of God, the presence of Being, the intimacy with the Ultimate and Gracious Mystery. A Hasidic phrase I came across the other day brought a bit of healing when it called for the wave (us) to wake up and realise that it is the ocean (the

Mystery of Love). We come into this world to align our souls with God, to realise that our very being is God's very being incarnate. We struggle to express these implications of Incarnation. The relationship between God and our souls is like that between the sun and its rays, between the wave and the ocean, between our breath and our life. We are the extension of God in time and space. I honestly believe that the current dis-ease of my body, my soul, my tumour, my mind are all somehow eased, soothed, settled a bit, by these small windows that open on to a much bigger and mysterious panorama of an astounding love and meaning.

Another tiny word, one we have lingered over many times in the past, can bring healing moments of a deeper meaning as it slips, unbidden, into an unfocused consciousness. It is the deceptively powerful word 'as'. AS. It almost sums up the eternal heart of Incarnation. God's only incarnate presence to me, now, is AS myself, *as* others, *as* nature! There is no God out there anymore. The Mystery is now, once and for all, fleshed – as you, as me, as everyone, as everything – especially right now as my tumour. The midnight journey is now further inwards into the dark cave, where, to our astonishment, we glimpse a hint of space and light and love.

Each time we sink a little more deeply into the infinite meaning of the word AS, another vibration of the healing understanding of our lives, of who we are, blossoms deeper still: we are truly created in the image and likeness of the Loving Creator. Nothing new here regarding another startling revelation: it's all to do with grasping it more profoundly, with 'getting it' more confidently, as the mystery of Incarnation gradually, in space and time, continues to come full circle. In ways beyond our imagination, this vision surely lifts the veil a little on the healing work of the Word in the world, and strangely, because of Incarnation, on the healing work of my tumour.

Richard Rohr believes that I can now enjoy God's flowing presence inside my own body, (1 Cor 3: 16-17) and I can love myself, others and God in the same flow. It is all the one Stream of Love.

Is this really true? And is it true that if I can truly accept my cancer it will bring healing? On the day I can truly love it, the world will be saved! "We do not initiate this process," Rohr goes on, "we only continue it. But it has to begin with some kind of healing understanding." For the umpteenth time I keep reminding myself, as the lights of passing cars chase each other across the ceiling, that this "healing understanding" is light years beyond a mere knowing *about* these spiritual things (which is where most of us fervent Catholics find ourselves, I fear), and more than the latest spiritual information that we store in our heads, (we go to talks, we buy books, we make retreats, we practice mindfulness). All of these activities are, of course, so useful, but only if they bring the one blessing that matters – the blessing of transformation. And do they? Do you sometimes wonder what kind of transformation your life is making in you?

Philosopher Ken Wilber writes of the true spiritual healing found when we finally understand something, enter the mystery a little and find its love and meaning. True spirituality touches "only a very, very small minority" he maintains. He is referring to "a radical transformation and liberation". The real function of religions and spirituality "does not fortify my separate self, but utterly shatters it – not consolation but devastation, not entrenchment but emptiness, not complacency but explosion, not comfort but revolution". This is a transmutation at the deepest seat of my self-awareness. What has all of this to do, I wonder, with my scabby, rash-covered chest, my itchy scalp, my tired and aching muscles? Healing? Deep meaning? Peace? These mornings I just cannot find the energy, the desire, the comfort of repeating by heart so many of the phrases, sayings, prayers that have helped me in the past to move with confidence and enthusiasm into the new day. Even though today I just haven't the heart for it, let me at least write one down for you. It came from the pen of a universal spiritual leader, Zen Master Thich Nhat Hanh:

Waking up this morning, I smile.
Twenty-four brand new hours are before me.
I vow to live fully in each moment, and to look
at all beings with eyes of compassion.

This morning I can only say, wryly, to the holy man 'Good luck with that!'

❦ 47 ❦

THE PERFECT DAY

I knew before I switched the light on that my face was blazing. I had been warned. The red, itchy and sore rash was spreading from my chest and back. Sore to the touch, this was another challenge to the ego. How will I 'face' the day, the people at Sunday Mass and the coffee afterwards? How would you feel about this? Or is it only me and my vanity? As one who has talked and written so much about depth, where was this depth now? My reactions floated on the slimy surface of stagnant water. How utterly pathetic! I bet you expected a more spiritual grounding, a more mature acceptance of the inevitable.

You may remember a story I used to tell about 'C', a socialite whose case was carried in the papers. She was, to the best of my memory, given an unusual court permission regarding the ending of her life, due to her utter failure to find a reason for living. In midlife the three dimensions of her social life that kept her buoyant had all diminished, now vanished: she was no longer the much-loved centre of attention, her considerable finances had run out, and her personal appearance, once stunning, had deteriorated drastically. She now had no alternative whatever as a reason for staying alive. The invincible power of the ego. I thought of that story this morning. And I wondered what reasons I now had for continuing to live.

I suppose no matter how well you know something theoretically, you do not really know it at all until you experience something of the situation at first hand. After all, to be suddenly knocked off your horse, to realise that the rest of your life, as you know it, is cancelled; that all your values and valuations of what 'success' is have no more meaning; that your health, proud fitness, freedom from pain or illness, your plans and projects are all over for ever: I suppose no one can ever be ready for such a shocking and savage introduction to the beginning of the end. Can you think of any of your heroines or heroes, people on whose wisdom you have relied, who have never crumpled in weakness and humiliation, before reaching that deeper and richer place? Not many. We Christians need think only of Jesus Christ our Saviour as the 'perfect' example of such a bloody destiny, yet we have such a weak and pitiful way of handling it.

I do not blame God for 'allowing' this upheaval to happen to me. Not for a moment. No more than a mother would allow anything to damage her child. She cannot protect her wee one from the risks of living, the situations that hurt, but she can love and comfort and make well again. So with God. Exactly the same. But do all lives have to be totally halted, utterly diminished, stripped and humiliated before they are deeply purified, their True North discovered, their True Selves at last revealed? Are these thoughts new for you, do you ever wonder about such matters, and how do you feel about them? Or is it better to get on with life and stop being so damn miserable?

One thing I must begin to do is settle for less in my daily life's expectation. Suddenly everything has become more immediate, the 'small' things have become extraordinarily important, fanciful dreams have disappeared over the horizon. 'A good day' is now assuming for me almost unrecognisable characteristics. To wake up with an intact stoma bag, to look in the mirror and find no new traces of disfigurement on my body, to manage a shower without swearing or scalding, to taste the porridge, to manage a smile, to think reasonably normally, to not fear the coming night. I remember reading in Solzhenitsyn's *One Day in the Life of Ivan Denisovich* his description of his perfect day. Among the reasons for his happiness was the fact that he had not picked up a cough or a cold after his long day in flimsy clothes in minus temperatures. And he had managed to smuggle a crumb of bread into the freezing camp for the night hunger. He had no expectations. Neither must I. Only a wholehearted co-operation with the inevitable!

☙ 48 ❧

WALKING THE PLANK

The worst morning yet. I feel at my lowest. Again forgive me for telling you the reasons. I've always been careful about my appearance, how I looked, how I dressed, how I watched my receding hairline. One friend called me 'Dan the Shirt', another 'Shiny Shoes'. Today I feel I must make a huge effort just to walk out the door of my flat and up the road into the village. There are new pimples on my face; it is pockmarked and I cannot shave. Neither can I swallow because of an ulcer on my tongue. My chest and back are unbearably sore, and sensitive to my clothes. My forebodings are deep. Can I carry this off: just to walk up the road?! I go through a thousand reasons for being able to perform this simple act; and another thousand about dying of shame. People will stare. I know they will. You may think I'm making a mountain out of a molehill. 'Oh come on!' I can hear you think, 'You do exaggerate!' You may feel that you yourself would come through this challenge with flying colours. I do not doubt that. But suffering is so notoriously relative. Those of you who know me fairly well will have the answer. It is fear, of course. Always is. I have prayed for courage all my life. You may have heard me say that it is God's favourite gift to us. In a few hours I will take some first steps up the road in another effort to experience it. While writing this (and I'm certainly not sure why I'm doing so) a thought has occurred to me:

I shall say hello today to all I meet. And if I know them reasonably well I shall talk about my face, and notice their compassionate reaction to my plight. There will be Hannah at the The StoryHouse, Chris at Costa's and Brenda at Sainsbury's.

As it happened, the first person was the District Nurse Sonja who had come to dress the PICC line. She wept when she saw me! Hannah understood my embarrassment at a glance! Her colleague Jerome advised me to grow a beard to cover the pimples, and to shave my head completely to divert attention from my face – strangely all of this banter put me at my ease a bit. Not as bad as I had feared. That evening I bought the new John Grisham novel, watched some rugby and opened a bottle of Rioja.

✵ 49 ✵

DEAR TUMOUR...

Oh holy tumour, I do not hate you, curse you or see you as the enemy. Like all of God's creatures, you too have lost your True North. But I do ask you to try to untwist the fibres of that deadly lump that has resulted in this disastrous blockage; it works against nature's wonderful way, and against God's loving desire.

Every cell in your structure is made of love. You have just taken a wrong turning (we all do), and assumed a false shape (we all do that too). With my left hand resting on my left side (where you are currently living), I press the blessings of my true nature and grace on the skin behind which you hide. This is God's blessing on you too. The Creator of Life weeps when you work against your nature, making the divine flow lose its way and take the wrong route.

Only love will melt the cold block at your centre. This will happen when you have achieved your precious gift hidden in your sudden intrusion into my unfolding life – the gift that is coming to me in pain, in sorrow, in the cross and in contradiction. Without you there are glimpses of understanding and wisdom I would otherwise have never known. That is why your flawed cradling, discovered a few months ago, is in fact a blessing – because somehow you are blessed by a God whose incarnation would have been impossible without fragile human flesh, all its vulnerabilities and a death. Remember those ramparts that surrender only to the most desperate tears and pain.

So, dear tumour, I thank you. Despite all appearances and initial fallout, you are still a true child of God's universe, of the mystery of Creation, yes, even of incarnate Love itself. If you feel it's time for your diminishment, even departure, your work completed, then so be it. I feel that soon your mission will be accomplished. And then the evolving pain-filled pattern of the Holy Spirit of Evolution will and must continue as before: death and life, always and everywhere. Your work done, true but imperfect nature will once again be your safe guide and facilitator. There will be one shining moment when the divine and human love and healing pouring from many hearts towards you each morning and every night, will slowly and surely, or maybe suddenly and finally, lessen your ambiguous presence and power for diminishment. This morning Big Des, another friend, sent me something his wife Linda had said, "He took the patches of his life and wove them into wings".

In you the cosmic and the personal meet, you are the bridge of paradox. At one stage Jesus could drink no more from the cup, then he once again reached out for it. He did not hate his cross; it was the death 'he freely accepted'. You, my tumour, are the death I must freely accept. The cup I must drink. I resist you with all my strength; yet I embrace you with love as well. You are a sublime mystery, as sublime, revealing, concealing and confusing as the Cross itself. You are the loaded dice the Creator threw nearly fourteen billion years ago. And now is your time. And mine too. There is no other way. We wish there were. And so, in a sense, must God. At the heart of Creation, and somewhere in the heart of each one of us, we feel the divine disappointment that suffering (and resistance) must happen, must keep spreading across God's incarnate body: as you do, now, across mine.

In the sad little poem *Making*, R.S. Thomas writes about God's delight in Creation and its first evolutionary stages where nature was obedient and the world was harmonious. The last lines are:

> *... Quickly the earth*
> *Teemed. Yet still an absence*
> *Disturbed me. I slept and dreamed*
> *Of a likeness, fashioning it,*
> *When I woke, to a slow*
> *Music; in love with it*
> *For itself, giving it freedom*
> *To love me; risking the disappointment.*[40]

But today, dear tumour, I have felt for a moment that the chemo-therapy is finding its way to your core. Today I sensed a small vibration of the invincible power of an incarnate God as it weaves its way between the cells that are only loosened by the fingers of a felt love. Today I sense a cosmic love-energy tentatively separating and reshaping, liberating and recalibrating, revising and resetting the original ground plan of evolutionary grace towards its True North, its final human and divine destiny.

Dear tumour, don't ask me how or why this happens, and in this way – the way of the cross. And the way of resurrection. I suspect that the intrinsic goodness of a divinely inspired Creation and Evo-lution, the innate love of each human and compassionate heart in prayer, the honed skills of medical men and women dedicated to the sacredness of every life, and the trust that believes in the astonishing, all-persuasive Love we call God expressed in these ways and many more. I suspect, dear tumour, that all these are the angels who will one day bring us two together to embrace, as we understand a little more of the secret love and meaning that lie at the mysterious heart of Creation and Incarnation.

❧ 50 ❧

HATING THE CHURCH

At low times in my life I am often somewhat disillusioned, even angry with the institutional Church that I've tried to serve, not brilliantly but the best way I could, over many decades. At the moment, with the sudden and severe changes in my daily life and the uncertainty and retrospections that go with it, together with the dreadful worldwide news about the secret evil at the heart of the R.C. Institution, I struggle against the real temptation to bitterness – an emotion I have always dreaded because of its cynical and poisonous hopelessness.

Some of the holiest people confess to similar sentiments, but they catch it in time. Carlo Carretto's story is well known. He combined a profound simplicity and love of the Church with an equally searing criticism of it. Am I at peace with what he wrote shortly before he died? Here is a short extract from it:

> *How much I must criticise you, my church, and yet how much I love you!*
> *How you have made me suffer much and yet I owe much to you.*
> *I should like to see you destroyed and yet I need your presence.*
> *You have given me much scandal and yet you alone have made me understand holiness.*
>
> *Never in this world have I seen anything more obscurantist, more compromised, more false, and yet never in this world have I touched anything more pure, more generous and more beautiful.*
> *Many times I have felt like slamming the door of my soul in your face*
> *– and yet how often I have I prayed that I might die in your sure arms!*[1]

Just now I cannot say I agree with his statement, nor can I follow the wild paradoxes in it. I do not see the Institutional Church along these lines. I believe it needs to be utterly stripped and re-founded. Or else we should prepare for a universal schism. During these months of my sometimes angry reflection, of my painful disillusionment, of my sharp criticism of the Institution's shocking male arrogance and triumphalism, I find comfort and trust, delight and healing only in the most beautiful face of the incarnate God, the true heart of the Christian faith. Only in that sacred, beating heart of the Human One can I find any acceptance of my cancer sentence, something that makes fragile sense of this purgatory, and a reason to worship and adore with every fibre of my being. An honest and mature mind can see both of Carretto's extremes, writer and teacher Fr Ronald Rolheiser reminds us. My mind does not stretch to that understanding or forgiveness at this time. Seems to me that Carretto wants to have his cake and eat it. Of course we all do.

❧ 51 ❧

FEELING THE FEAR

It's already mid-September – three months of experiencing unfamiliar forests, deserts and swamps for body, heart and mind. Had I expected to escape the crucible of life, the night times of my days? Did I imagine I would never feel really shattered and broken? "What woman, what man," asks Santorelli, "can deny this inescapable reality somewhere in their life, and still hope to become a human being in the fullest sense of the term?"[42] The lists of such unfathomable, unwanted, sudden and dreaded intrusions are many and varied: the sudden death of a loved one; the loss of a job or a dream; the return of a memory that still springs up to haunt our nights; or, in my own situation, the revelation of a malignant cancer that blows open the fragility, dependency and vulnerability of the rest of my life.

Only this morning, for instance, I was shocked at the extent of the mess and mistakes of my now utterly changed daily to-do lists, for example my medication timetable. My weakened mind was unable to identify, remember and allocate certain tablets at certain times. All the little boxes and pills, counted out so carefully the night before, yet now so utterly mixed up in my scrambling mind. And then other examples flooded my mind that have occurred since I began this nightmare experience. How swiftly fear can fill us! How easily it shrinks our hope and dims our light. Toxic thoughts around dementia filled my anxious mind this morning; and then, fuelled by negative oxygen, the exaggerations began. Are these fearful thoughts true?

Only a hard-earned habit of quiet sitting and contemplation will help me at this point. There are times when repeated mantras, internal affirmations and denial of the negative emotions will not suffice to shift the darkness – a key factor in the healing is to realise that the light lies hidden in the experience of fear itself. To be with the fear, to be inside it, to feel it rather than to deny, dismiss, attack or try to banish it. This requires a fierce and intense surrender by which I try to lose myself in trust and faith. The wise ones tell us that this kind of courage opens up the heart, and the hearts of others, to that free and open place in us (in me) that is always compassionate, invincibly loving and full of comforting angels. From our past conversations, you may remember that this courageous surrender is that place of inner authority, of my most authentic presence to the 'really real'. It is from there that I may one day start living again...

52

THE WEE POINT OF FRACTURE

"The wee point of fracture," scholar William Barclay believes, is where love and fear meet; where faith and the total loss of it coincide; where grace is replaced by huge doubt; where the black dog-elephant in the room of my soul must speak out. What is that shadow for me right now? What is it for you today? Is our pain the price we pay for our individual sins, to win our personal peace and salvation, as we were brought up to believe, or is it, asks Merton, to help hold the suffering of the world in a healing way? When the incoming crashing waves of love are dashed against the immovable shores of denial and disbelief, when the hopes of relief encounter the cold cliffs of doubt: is that the pain of losing faith that happened to Jesus, too, during the last minutes of his life. Where are the angels in my Gethsemane garden? Today a good friend John Sullivan sent me an email, "There is no being found without our being lost first (and often). And if there's no intimacy, there's no ultimacy. They are integrally related. In this case, illness like Jean's and yours exposes us to forms of intimacy and helplessness that are new, unwelcome, debilitating, which rob us of our past sense of dignity, even identity. New aspects of intimacy hover around us in such moments. But, whether we feel it or not, we *are* swimming in a sea of grace."

As I searched around for some meaning in my pain I discovered that Evelyn Underhill believed that the heart of suffering requires a definite plan of life; and a courage in sticking to that plan, not for months or years but for life. New mental and emotional habits and values must be formed, and all our interests radically rearranged around a new centre. Even on small issues and personal levels this will cost a good deal. For me now, it just seems an impossible task. I do not want to be a victim like many of the saints were, or to be a true follower of Jesus. It is much easier to be a worshipper of him, to shout my 'Alleluias' at a safe distance from commitment and involvement, to go to (or say) Mass rather than be crucified into a new and demanding way of living and loving.

Our lives as Catholics are so often a delight to our ego. We draw back when we begin to realise the "costing not less than everything" of Eliot.[43] Was this the cost for the special martyrs - or for all of us? Does this requirement cross your mind often? Or at all? We cannot bear to lose the love of the world, to part with our present desires, tastes and lifestyles; we go for our occasional 'spiritual top-up' and think we are already in the thick of some kind of spiritual dying. In reality, we are mostly well satisfied to remain as we are; it is only our conscience we want taken away!

Basil Hume reminded us that the demands of Jesus crucify us. Not only when we are asked to take up those small crosses every day, or even edgier, more serious ones: like being publicly humiliated, rubbished, written off, a failure, seen as inadequate and disrespected by others. What I feel now seems to be in another place, a place of numbness as I leave one way of being for another, plus the whole reorientation of my life from one world to another. The wise and holy comments of our spiritual sisters and brothers fall on the stony soil of my heart and mind in this season of my life. Walking away seems like a good idea. On rereading all of this, I ask you again, dear reader, to please remember that these thoughts and feelings are flooding in through the breaches in my clerical wall of protection when the shock of cancer strikes without warning. Why do we have to wait for accidents, incidents, shocks and tragedies (like cancer) to happen before we realise the shallowness and emptiness of our seemingly religious lives?

❧ 53 ❧

THE DUST THAT DREAMS OF GLORY

God with a stoma bag, scratching the rash, vomiting in the toilet, flushing tufts of hair down the sink. Humanity is God living dangerously! Incarnation is a risky business for the Creator. Becoming human is asking for trouble, and God certainly found it. At Holy Communion we put on God's skin for others and God puts on our skin for others too. We become that vulnerable 'self-in-God; God is the self-in-us'. I am that weak point of fracture. Just as I am these months, full of emptiness and real or imagined loss, I am, unbelievably, part of God's incarnate presence, part of the divine becoming flesh, a speck of dust that dreams of glory.

In my daily anxiety, constant apprehension, deepening fear, God is somehow becoming more incarnate in the world. And in my struggling with the cross, I am becoming more and more a living sacrament in a world of a million sacraments, where everything is always dying to itself to live, more purified, in a truer shape and substance of God's ever-emerging presence in, and as, all that exists, experiences and evolves. The world spins around the cross and the spinning force is the energy of Easter. The Blessed Trinity dances across the universe and the universe is the fourth person of the dancing set.

In my thinking I imagine all the pain in the world, of which I feel myself to be a small part just now, in a fire of energy, and watch it renewing the world: great suffering and great love. We cannot deny this revelation. Our central Christian image of love is the destroyed body of an outcast dripping blood from a crude cross; this, we are told, is the focus of the fire that is redeeming the world. How we struggle to get a line on this! How strange a mystery that God's most precious gifts, when incarnated, emerge as the most significant suffering? And how strange a mystery it is that, devoid of my pain, I may have missed life's richest experience of God incarnate; a pain, in fact, that may well be the greatest language of the soul! Does it bring me any consolation, in my 3.00am dreaded fear, that God is, at this moment "breaking me down to his own oblivion, to send me forth on a new morning, a new man"?[44] Or that "I live now, not I, but my suffering incarnate God lives within me"? (Gal 2: 20). Or that, through this fiery unbidden cauldron of confusion, we are, actually, becoming one, falling into an ever-more total alignment with each other, a fusing together of ourselves with our universe, into a greater Love? Does all or any of this sustain me as I wait for the dawn? Frankly no! There are times when the raw cries of the hurting heart will not be comforted by the religious logic of the cold mind.

⚘ 54 ⚘

HOLD ON, PLEASE!

Don't let go! Don't give up until you understand the astonishing story more clearly. Stay awake for that glimpse of the mystery of who you are, of the master plan that surrounded your birth and baptism with a God's love. Do not abandon your search for meaning, for the wisdom that is called Sophia. How do we begin to grasp the love-story of Creation and Incarnation, of our Mother God's love for everyone and everything, of the primal energy of the Holy Spirit at the heart of our evolving world? Find time each day to think of all that calls out the inner essence, the primal energy, the very truth and love between people and in nature. It is found everywhere – in every person and in every thing. Then think of the mother whose deepest self is growing, evolving and taking shape and substance within her body. She is the beginning, middle and end of another life, her baby's; within her and then without her. She is not completely one with her baby; but neither are they two. Given this intimacy between mother and baby, Incarnation tells us that God's love is not just more intense and complete than such a mother's love. It reveals that this creative moment actually *is* God's love amongst us; the mother-baby relationship is revealed *as* the incarnate divine way of unique and fleshy presence in our midst.

We are created in the very image and likeness of our Mother God, moved by an overpowering and overflowing love. From the start, we are inseparably and objectively at one with the flaming heart of an unconditionally loving Lover. Religions, doctrines and Christian teachings have resisted this truth with a deadly tenacity, emphasising Augustine's "original sin" and his description of humanity as a "damned mass" in which only sin is transmitted in marital intercourse, Calvin's "total human depravity" and Luther's references to human beings as "piles of filth". Millions cannot rise above these destructive beliefs, or climb out of those pits of nihilism. Strains of such a sinful and heretical teaching are still visible in many Christian churches such as our own Roman Catholic institution. Pope Francis is doing all he can to condemn such destructive doctrines. Richard Rohr asks whether we can ever undo such foundational damage and messages of damnation. During the times I cannot sleep or read because of emotional fatigue and low spirits, my mind runs all over the place and these thoughts about Christians' resistance to the most beautiful love-story makes me so sad, so helpless.

Once we discover and believe the astonishing secret of the love at the heart of all Creation, then all we have to do is to follow the flow of that river, to till the fertile soil, knowing that the Indwelling Spirit has already been planted within, and will remind us of all we need to remember, to know and to cherish. We have just seen how many doctrines around sin and redemption have been seriously misunderstood, leaving the true story radically lost and almost impossible to resurrect. Sinners we may well be – but we did not start out as sinners. Separateness and disconnection came later. All began in the closest union; then the lies began to be told. This is surely a time for tears.

🎍 55 🎍

ALREADY LOVED

I have already mentioned the healing I find in glimpses of meaning and true revelation, that holistic sense of well-being that happens when I understand things a little more clearly, when something of the revelation I was born to hear reaches the depths of my heart. During the nights, the early mornings, those tired middays, I linger over these amazing but blurred insights, especially one - that I do not have to do anything to reach greater union with God because I'm already there, already 'got it' as Rohr would say. "Before the world began you were lovingly and delightedly chosen, chosen in Christ to live through love in his presence." (Eph 1: 4) I do not have to find a way forward into the divine embrace: all I have to do is to reconnect with that Infinite Source, to be awakened to the true but forgotten milieu where I'm always essentially living, but asleep. Like belonging to my family, I cannot get there; I do not need to; I can only *be* there. I already utterly and totally belong to that nest of love. There is no need to start all over again. Christ has taken care of everything. Resurrection is already ours. Like holy spiders of the Spirit we are always invisibly weaving the webs of love between hearts and across planets.

Even when tormented by my new demons, even when the likely long-term prognosis gets more ominous, there is something in my psyche that is lifted by love. Knowing that I am the child of divine love, that love is my beginning, my sustenance and my end, can pierce the carapace of an ever-threatening despair. In the wee small hours, even as a howling autumn wind blows in from where the Mersey estuary meets the Irish Sea, the whisper of our loving genesis can ease the grip of fear. Like the murmur of a far wave the reminder of our need to love and to be loved, and that this is so, can prepare me for the long night ahead.

To be reminded that I am deeply, truly loved, that I have mattered to many, that in every breath, every step, every heartbeat, every thought, every stuttered 'yes' I manage, I'm completing God's image and likeness in me, the divine-becoming-human even as the human is revealed as divine, is so unbelievably beautiful. And it is beauty that saves and renews us, that keeps the fragile balance during our moody blues, that keeps the tipping-point tipping in the right direction. To love and be loved; to know and be known. Otherwise my life is a distortion, a defacing, a de-incarnating of that most wonderful divine birthmark and image that filled and shaped my birth, that waits to be perfected by God's creative power immanently present in all my experiences. Slowly and surely, the love that saturates my very being will change, heal and complete everything. In his *Late Fragment* poet Raymond Carver wrote:

> *And did you get what*
> *You wanted from this life, even so?*
> *I did.*
> *And what did you want?*
> *To call myself beloved, to feel myself*
> *Beloved on the earth.*[45]

❧ 56 ❧

GREAT SUFFERING; GREAT LOVE (1)

It's four months since the cancer diagnosis. It's the fourth cycle of chemotherapy; the fourth visitation of the searing side-effects of the cetuximab drug. I began today to wonder about others, like me, who are rebuilding and readjusting their thinking around their changed lives. There has been no shortage of advice, examples and well-intentioned stories from a large group of friends and acquaintants. These include miracle cures that verge on the alarming, strange diets and exercises that many people utterly believe in.

Many stories reveal extraordinary courage and perseverance, an unshakeable optimism and faith of some kind; others, maybe like me, experience mainly only nights of near-despair. There were those who found some kind of peace in many deep conversations with their friends; there were those who avoided such communications as much as possible; and there were those who were very selective regarding who they shared with, and how much they shared. Some never let up the search for distractions, legitimate and very temporary diversions, small pleasures to look forward to; others made no such efforts, having already connected their cancer with an impending death. Many wrote that while they did not really fear death itself, it was 'the complicated road of treatment' that threatened them; they 'feared death less than they feared the doctors!' they admitted.

I have, however, noticed one very significant difference in how people who suffer from cancer talk or write about it. This caught my attention big time and made me ask myself many profound questions. And this difference was discernible also in those who would call themselves believers, or describe themselves as being religious, mostly of the Christian persuasion. I'm referring to those 'victims' who regard their cancer as an assault on their lives, their health, their future. There are believers, and other-than-believers, who use a military kind of language and imagery to emphasise their approach to the situation, seeing cancer as the aggressor, the attacker, the silent assassin.

Such personal reflections will contain words and phrases such as 'the enemy gathering strength for another assault', and 'needing a heavy bombardment of chemo'. Also about 'preparing for battle' and 'depriving the cancer of victory'. Or needing 'a cease-fire with the nasty opponent'. I suppose there's no big deal here, but I do want to outline another way of envisioning the whole situation, especially when we bring God into the equation. A whole lot depends on whether we see God as 'out there somewhere' or whether we understand God as the essential life, energy and being of everything that happens in an evolving planet and humanity.

Without unnecessarily confusing the issue, I feel sure that how we see and understand our cancer, how we reflect and pray about it, will be deeply influenced by the kind of theology and spirituality we already hold about everything: our lives, our suffering, our blessings, our death, our relationships, every experience. All is grace. (I tried to outline my whole stance to these vital issues in my recent book *An Astonishing Secret* and its accompanying online video course.) However, since I am now actually experiencing the terrible ordeal of dealing with cancer, and dealing with it badly maybe, and not just writing about it, I am shocked at the difference between my past 'good and holy thoughts' about the experience, and the terrible, raw and relentless reality of it now.

57

GREAT SUFFERING; GREAT LOVE (2)

Some serious evangelical and dualistic devotees would see God as utterly unconnected with the flow of ordinary, evolving life, often interrupting the unfolding way of things, responding favourably to certain prayers, rituals, pilgrimages and devotion to particular saints. Moreover, miracles are needed by those who campaign for the canonisation of very holy people. There are many good reasons for asking God to change the natural course of our lives: to protect the harvest for hungry and desperate people, to ease the suffering, to restore peace to war-torn nations and conflicted communities. Yet, because Incarnation is my life's lodestar, I always try to understand, honour and respect the seamless flow of loving energy that I believe is God's chosen way of living radically present in us, and that permeates all life and death at the deepest levels. That is why, even in my weakest and most desperate moments I find I cannot beg of God to change that natural and supernatural way of evolutionary being, and to zap or blast away chunks of my tumour because I cannot figure out where God begins and the tumour ends. (See no 49 'Dear Tumour')

Would your approach, like most people's, be to 'destroy the aggressor' that you believe God wishes destroyed too, to see it as a contradiction of what your life should be; or would your approach be to identify with that disguised, incarnate God of all being, with that love, whose very meaning lies in the unfolding and experiencing of the light and dark of what awaits us each day? Because it is there, and there only, I believe, that we come face to face with our destiny, our True Self, our true home. This significant difference of approach to the question of my cancer will depend on how deep my understanding of God's love is, of how I grasp the mystery of creation, of the theology of Incarnation, of the hidden reality and secret power of my suffering.

But basically, do we see everything, every person, every question, every experience, every reality – with not one exception – as wrapped in, infused by, marinated in, disguised in, fired and sustained by the purest and most beautiful love? In short, Richer Rohr asks us to contemplate on the twin truths of *great suffering* and *great love*. And, as I try to make sense of my radically altered life, I still find I cannot curse the tumour or do anything with it except doggedly ask God to reveal its lesson, to open my being to it, and, in his mercy, to bring about its promised, deepest and traumatic transformation. And that is the transformation into the very essence and being, the very breath and heartbeat of the Love we call God.

The mornings here near the window are cold now. Winter has clearly claimed the North West of the UK. And so I try to gather my thoughts in terms of this suffering and love in my deepest being. First of all, to begin with the *great suffering*, I can safely say that my current life, as a chemo zombie, is a mass of pain. Every thought, movement and silence is sliced through with some kind of suffering: a soreness that is embossed, like a shadow, through every moment of mind, heart and body. There is no need to repeat the litany of this state – from the spiritual loss, the emptiness, the fear, the depression, the invisible tears, the end of all my plans for the years to come, and the dullness of spirit, to the physical challenge of every 'normal' chore: getting out of bed, dressing, washing, eating, showering, medicating, finding enough energy to face another bag-change, combing my scabby head, dozing through another slow day – and then another night. In there, in all of that, is more suffering than I have ever endured.

And then there is the *great love*. The great love I refer to is, of course, God's love. There is no love in me as a separate entity. Everything loving in my heart is the divine love incarnate. None of it is my own, so to speak. Only as much as I'm open to, ready for, can hold. I tend to link this 'great love' with the courage it takes to live each day as 'normally' as possible. I bless myself with holy water before I leave the flat to go to the village for shopping, for the daily paper, maybe for a cup of coffee and a Bakewell tart. I watch the face of the barista or the server or the checker-out and wonder have they noticed the new red rashes on my face, the thinning hair, the pathetic efforts to fake 'normal'; are they feeling pity for me? I do not really know. But this I do know – my ego is alive and well.

❦ 58 ❦

GREAT SUFFERING; GREAT LOVE (3)

I try also to see everything through the lens of *a great love*. Everything. The chemo regime is the loving will of God. The consultant's detailed outlines of my day are also the maternal embrace of my Divine Creator's reaching arms. There is no space between nature and grace. Nature *is* the grace. Grace can only work in us *as* nature. The ordinary *is* the extraordinary. Matter is always inseparably fused with the Holy Spirit. For the Christian, love is just everywhere. It is the oxygen of the universe; it is the substance of each breath, the energy of each heart's murmur. Even the waves of fog that swirl around between my soul and mind tonight will be deciphered and decoded by love in the morning. And so will each toss and turn as I anxiously negotiate space for my new bedfellows – the stoma bag, the chemo bottle, the PICC line and a few hankies – they all reveal the deeper love that drives everything towards its completion.

The Holy Spirit is the love-energy of each tremor of suffering, each tumour of threat, each birth-pain of becoming, each wrench of loss. It is only through our dying – our body-pain, our soul-pain, our planet-pain – that we will ever understand the length and depth of the divine love-pain. Nothing exists outside love. That is why I believe my bowel tumour is such a special gift: without it there are expanses of light and truth and wisdom that I would never have experienced. There is a sense in which to reject my cancer is to reject God, to reject love. Every time I fall into severe doubts about such truth I beg for a deeper understanding of the Incarnation. Everything I think of these days, everything I write, everything expressed in my recent *An Astonishing Secret* is, to my mind, at the heart of Christian Incarnation.

Falling in love with a tumour is no easy matter. And yet, that is what I, as a Christian, am called to do. Practicing Catholics have been doing it ever since they were children: reaching for the Good Friday cross, embracing and kissing it; finding a seamless love amidst the nails and splinters; glimpsing the tender eyes of God made human in the agonised face of Jesus; learning how to love no matter what. Only great suffering will take us so deeply into love; only great love will hold us during the days and nights of such great suffering. No matter how deeply I slide, or plunge, into my personal, cold abyss, God will always already be there, warm with love; and waiting. To this principle there are no exceptions.

And not just on the personal level. Love is also the energy of the entire universe. "Deep in our DNA," writes Rohr, "we belong to the stars, the trees and the galaxies. We belong to one another because we have the same source of love; the love that flows through the trees is the same love that flows through my being..." Dylan Thomas expresses this interfusion of nature and grace as only the poet can:

> *The force that through the green fuse drives the flower*
> *Drives my green age...*
> *The force that drives the water through the rocks*
> *Drives my red blood...*[46]

❦ 59 ❦

COMMENTS OF OTHERS

When my energy and available time came together, I tried to find out more about how people react to their encounters and diagnosis of cancer. I found many variations. I compared them with my own, some very different, some quite similar. There is no right reaction, no wrong way. You will wonder too about how you might meet this moment if it ever touches your life; and for one in every three or four, it will. One common observation was about the close link between bodily health and meditation. The fitter you are, many believed, the more care you have taken of your body throughout your life, the better chance you have of recovering your health and coming safely through. 'You've kept fit,' I'm often challenged, 'yet you've got cancer!' That is true. But maybe it would all have happened much sooner, and much more severely if I hadn't. Or so two of the consultants told me.

Another remark that stayed with me was from someone who saw the painful process as 'practising dying'. I was attracted to that comment because I believe it. I would add that it is also a version of 'practising living'. When I think about it carefully, the way I live my life when death is ominously close is also the way I should live my life when all is well. Like Jesus did, I too must die many times before the final call. As the cancer spreads and bites more intrusively, bit by bit I must let go of some more of my freedoms each day, with a gradual diminishing and handing over that carry either the bitter weight of death or the lasting lightness of life. As chaplain to hospitals I have marvelled at those who manage, gracefully, to let go, and learn quickly to 'practise dying,' and I have prayed my heart out for those who find it impossible to surrender anything of their lives or lifestyles for any reason. That we *grow by subtraction* is a hard lesson to learn.

In my reading around cancer and grace I can understand the writer who refuses to really share with anyone who has not endured the experience of having cancer themselves. Well-meaning and sincere, I find little comfort in the platitudes of those who wish to lighten my load; for example, 'I know *exactly* how you feel!' How can they? A common fault is to presume that all kinds of cancer and all kinds of human constitutions are fundamentally much the same. Consolers 'know somebody' who 'came through' in no time at all. And most weeks I get news of, or small bottles of, miracle cures of dubious origins and results.

For many contributors, among the disturbing elements of the experience of having cancer were the unwelcome insights they had into what they were like deep down: a cranky control freak, a selfish, self-centred and demanding 'patient'. This is a rude awakening for one's self-satisfied self-awareness. I began to realise for the first time how petty and evasive I can be, how difficult I am as a companion, how I see everything in terms of 'how does this affect me'. A fairly common remark by those who had gone through the trials of hosting cancer concerns a tight privacy, a kind of fear and ambiguity about telling others the full story of their condition. Writers who have or had had cancer wondered about who to tell, and how much they should reveal. Some just let it all out; most only became more open as their condition got worse. A few confessed to a tentative positive acceptance of their shocking news; the majority had nothing good whatever to say about that news.

Either way, people wrote of a whole raft of moods, energies, emotions and profound reflections. Most were very slow to appear utterly hopeless and helpless, or to mention the word 'depression'. As we have seen earlier in these reflections, whether or not to stop the chemo, and when and why to do so, was also a common topic in these personal accounts I'm referring to. Some patients never call a halt to treatment; others do after one or two courses especially if the side-effects are almost unbearable. So much depends on the quality of life without the chemo treatment. I often think and pray about this option. It is a very sobering time of discernment. And again, some writers seemed to be able to make this momentous decision fairly easily and serenely. They seemed to be empowered by their deeply personal relationship with Jesus, or some Spirit of Life, maybe God; by walking and talking with him, by looking and listening to him. They cease their note-making, their journaling, their recording – and, in the lovely imagery of John Moriarty, they "go the soul's way" in good time. John wished these words to be read at his funeral a few years ago:

> *Clear mornings bring the mountains to my doorstep.*
> *Calm nights give the rivers their say.*
> *Some evenings the wind puts its hand on my shoulders.*
> *I stop thinking; I leave what I'm doing,*
> *And I go the soul's way.*[47]

❦ 60 ❦

IF ONLY ...

Every week I look at my diary to mull over where I should be in my itinerary of retreats and talks were I not nobbled by cancer. The pages of venues and dates are criss-crossed out and a new agenda of hospital appointments for chemo courses, scans and consultancy sessions written in. Each week I miss those beautiful places and trusting people who gather in many retreat centres, mainly now in Ireland and England, for meditation, spiritual inputs, silence, intense sharing and 'inner work'. Cancelling all of them, at great inconvenience and financial loss for the centres and participants, broke my heart.

And each venue has its own special memory. This week, for instance, I would have been at spectacular Dromantine in Newry. One year I was there in April when the row of cherry trees by the lake were completing their blossoming, one by one, day by day, as we prayed our way through the week with the title '"Speak to us of God, O cherry tree". And the cherry tree blossomed'. It was a moment when the sublime Artist's delicate touch painted and sculpted all around us the intimacy and unity of nature and grace, of Creation and Incarnation, of the Holy Spirit and Evolution. Our Eucharistic symbols and prayers each day tried to intensify and imprint in our souls the incarnate beauty being played out before the bewildered and delighted gaze of our astonished hearts.

Part Four

❦ 61 ❦

THE STARE

"Who is watching me?" I'm here at the This Is Livin restaurant in Crosby Village writing what you are now reading. I ask this question because I looked in the mirror the moment I got up today. My face was terrible with red blisters, yellow scabs, sore patches and rashes, nose and lips that are cracking open and very painful. I'm now slow to lift up my head and look around me. "Who is watching me?" The walk from my flat to here is called Blundellsands Road East. This morning it felt like a 'way of the cross' as I tried to avoid meeting or greeting anybody, avoiding all eye-contact. It was a real taste of the dying we are called to undergo, a touch of the desperation that fills my soul.

I pause here to wonder about what you yourself may be thinking about just now. If you have not actually experienced something similar to what I'm describing, then you may not find what I am writing pertinent. You will probably judge me as making a fuss about something or nothing. One day in the future I may feel the same way about this morning. But please remember, I'm only telling the story as I feel it at the time. During that walk to the village I found myself imagining the healing effect of suddenly meeting my long-departed mother who would bless my mess of a face with her beautiful look of love, who would kiss away the shame, embarrassment and fear. (How often have I heard stories about how even the toughest war veterans have called out for their mother in the face of fear, desperation or death.) Who would have thought that these strange thoughts were haunting my mind as I walked along in fear, yet trying to whistle a happy, but rather pathetically flat tune?

✤ 62 ✤

ONLY CONNECT!

Our wisest people keep insisting on the healing power of connecting things in our minds, of trying to complete some fragments of life's mystery as we experience it. You may have noticed this connecting dimension of my illness as expressed in these pages. How to see my personal pain as part of the universal and incarnate, beloved and broken presence of the Risen Christ, or of the free Holy Spirit at work and at play across the painfully evolving heart of the cosmos and across the equally painfully evolving cosmos of my heart? How do I lose my smaller existence so as to find the abundant life, to read my present pain through the lens of the bigger picture of an evolving universe: "I live now not I, but a greater Life possesses me."?

Within the last year I wrote *An Astonishing Secret: the Love Story of Creation and the Wonder of You.* It was full, for me at least, of vital, spiritual connections and clarifying mental observations. It was also completed before cancer struck, when my mind was clear and my health was enviable. Trying to create those healing connections just now, in the middle of my troubled nights, at the gut-level of pain and visceral reality, is a very different task. As I tried to explain in the introduction to the content of this book, the effort here is to meditate on suffering primarily from the felt experiences of heart and body as well as from the cerebral perspectives of the mind.

May I mention again, by way of a brief summary, some central themes and topics around connecting. Try to bring the Zen wisdom of *Beginner's Mind* to what follows. Let go of all that brainwashing that so poisoned our early lessons about God. Take first steps into another place and any one of them will open up many more paths into the mystery. And notice that all of them are interwoven with paradox and contradiction. In a confused way we are sometimes gifted with glimpses through a glass darkly – a healthy challenge to much of the indoctrination about God and Creation by the teaching Institution of the Church of our youth. A huge revolution and revelation is now afoot. Our constant emphasis on Incarnation is leading us to beautiful insights. One concerns the revelation of the connection between *Matter* and *Spirit*. Only it is not about connecting, but something infinitely closer. It is to the graced *fusion* of the two that Incarnation testifies. You just cannot have one without the other. It is the origin, foundation and ultimate destiny that is the love and meaning at the heart of Christianity. No other religion does it as well.

❧ 63 ❧

MATTER AND SPIRIT

"Spirit always desires to incarnate itself." That is how Richard Rohr puts it. Translated into my current cancer condition it would mean that something truly divine is taking place in the growing or shrinking of my tumour. This understanding of our faith is, of course, as old as the hills. (And we are rarely reminded of it!) As Christians we should be identified by our 'visceral' attitude to Incarnation, and the paradox of suffering. Just notice the context and weaving of light and dark in the Infancy and Passion narratives. Rohr's summary also expresses God's desire to live at the heart of our pain, to become, in Jesus, the divine/human back to bear and carry our particular crosses.

There is something in the burden of my present condition which fiercely fleshes divine and most tender love. There is no other way for Incarnation to happen, to break down my wilful ego, to reveal a deeper truth. How strange a mystery that God's most precious gift, when incarnated, emerges as suffering! In my mental and bodily crucifixion this morning I'm taking part in a painful identification with the Christian God. Rohr keeps reminding us that sooner or later life is going to lead us into a place of pain we cannot fix, control, explain or understand. That's where transformation most readily happens, he believes, because only then, and there, are we finally and completely in the hands of God. We are helpless and powerless in the face of our darkness.

All of this could be called the essence of the human condition. And it needs much contemplation to understand that life-transforming revelation. And there is a certain urgency about that call. The above "life-transforming revelation" is both personal and universal; it begins with Creation and leads to Incarnation. Remember again the words of St Thomas Aquinas, "If we get Creation wrong we get God wrong". The following approach has helped me to glimpse what he meant and make more sense of my faith:

Not so long ago people believed that the earth was the centre of all Creation. The sun went around it; it was all complete and fixed. Now we know that it belongs to a galaxy called the *Milky Way* and that there are millions of other galaxies out there in space, all with trillions of planets. Our earth is but a grain of sand on the shores of the universe; our sun is but one among billions of stars – many of which may well be inhabited by some kind of intelligent life. Social media carries daily revelations of the astonishing evolution in the realms of science. We struggle even to imagine the meaning and implications of all that is going on. We need to begin a new expansion of our imagination, to start seeing things from a radically new perspective. (I have tried to express my glimpses of the mystery in *An Astonishing Secret*.)

Too many of us, for instance, continue to believe in a God who is too small and separate from us – confined to a remote heaven or to this religion or that, a punishing God, a judgemental God that many of us were told about when we were children! Much of this was destructive indoctrination that made a loving relationship with God practically impossible in later life for millions of us. Moreover, many Christians still hold the image of God as 'someone out there'. But there is no God out there. Is it too much to picture God as the enduring love and energy behind, beneath and within all things? When you pause to reflect on the mystery of yourself, of Incarnation, do you sometimes sense that there is a profound, invisible presence in every star, every breath, every moment and event, at the heart of every experience? A face of love, a smile of reassurance, holding everyone and everything together in delightful ways we cannot even imagine?

❦ 64 ❦

LOVE-IMAGES

Occasionally in the middle of my restlessness and worry I will reach for a pen and a page to take my mind off the situation I want to deny. I find a blessed relief in mulling over the love-story of Incarnation, ruminating on the forgotten theological and spiritual teachings, and their implications for our lives and that of our precious world. And so, in the lovely light of these thoughts in many of these pages, we need, I'm certain, new images for God. What might these images be? Maybe a Mother God who is deeply in love with us, a Lover God who adores us, our names branded on her hands, an Artist God who designed, created and sustains the whole of Creation and its astonishing beauty, and who loves it unconditionally, no matter what. A key concept here, too, is that God is simply another name for unconditional love. This is a love we cannot change in the slightest way, no matter what; a love that never sleeps, keeping the time and tune, as Dante wrote, of the cosmic dance of sun and stars.

Or, for instance, ask yourself about how you understand the mystery of the Incarnation. Every word of this book, and this project, tries to open our hearts, and to present the astonishing image of the irrepressible love of God. Referring to God and Creation, Pope Francis recently spoke of the divine impulse and imperative to create and spread unconditional love. And that's why God created the world and us – so that Incarnation would happen. (As we keep saying, it was happening from the beginning: the Big Bang was the first incarnation.) From the beginning God was in love with us and wanted to live among us, *and as us*, to reveal to us what true humanity looks like. God became like us so that we would become like God. The humanity of God; the divinity of us. Both so perfectly present in Jesus, the Human One.

To repeat. Once more! This beautiful spirituality reveals that nothing went wrong with God's Creation. There never was an angry God who banished us from a garden because of an original sin by Adam and Eve. Paradise was not lost: because it never existed. There was only ever Plan A, never a Plan B of God's original desire going wrong, of atonement and reparation by what St Augustine described as a *massa damnata*. Creation was for Incarnation to take place; it was never about the *mea culpas* of guilt. Creation was the preparation for Jesus; God has never been disappointed with us for any original sin: only always delighted with us, exactly as we are. I remind myself that God never ever punishes anybody for anything. God just cannot punish or send us trials. Unconditional love is the meaning of the word 'God'.

The divine name is a verb, not a noun. God does not really give her conditional love and forgiveness; unconditional love and forgiveness is what God essentially *is*. Please try to interiorise this wisdom without the slightest doubt. Your heart already knows this well, so believe it, trust it. Everything, somehow, is love. As the demons draw near, and every morning they do, I try to protect myself in the shadow of what I know by heart: that our deepest reality is love. Can you think of a better way to pray, a better way of touching our Lover's tender heart, than to be meditating, lingering and delighting in these truths; especially when the darkness is heavy, and formal prayers may not help anymore? Is there a more sustaining way of preparing for an unknown and precarious future; a better way of anticipating the final intimacy with God that we long for, that we were created for?

65

THE SEAMLESS LOVE-WEB OF THE SPIRIT AND EVOLUTION

Much of all this is challenging and confusing, but only because it is different from what we were often (very erroneously) told. It is the heart of our faith but in a new language and imagery. It is worth all the energy and passion we can muster to understand it more profoundly. This theology tries to tell the Christian Story in terms of a deep and endless love: always flowing from within, the work of the Holy Spirit; always emerging, since the first Creation, from deep within. As an example: think of a seed, going through all the stages of growing, changing, blossoming. Everything it needs for its final flourishing is already within it. Everything, *everything*, is already within. Notice how this changes your understanding of God, of Creation, of the Love-Story at the heart of Christianity.

Now think, for instance, of the Evolution of Creation, the gradual gestation of God's own incarnate being. As we have emphasised earlier, there never was an historic Adam and Eve, no 'fall', no punishment, no atonement; this story is meant to be understood as a worthy myth about the human condition. The mistake in taking it literally leaves a terrible legacy of destruction for God's people; a damaging legacy that is still not admitted or corrected but remains entrenched in our catechisms and doctrines. The true story is only one long love-story. Hear it as the Holy Spirit speaking to you, to all humanity, to the world, to an evolving Creation. It is the only and true Gospel story. This is how St Paul puts it: "You yourselves are God's love-letters... written not with ink but with the Spirit of the living God, not on tablets of stone but on the pages of your living, loving hearts." (2 Cor 3: 3)

Here is another glimpse of the delightful mystery of Spirit-filled Evolution. The love and light in the First Flaring forth, the Big Bang, the first Incarnation, the first Bible, is the same light and love that guides every subsequent evolutionary breakthrough on Planet Earth; the same light that saw the emergence of human self-consciousness; the same love that drew forth from the womb of the Earth and of Mary, the final, fleshed reason for Creation in the first place – the Incarnation of God in the human Jesus – in whom this whole Love Story was finally revealed.

It continues to be revealed every day when the sun rises, every day when a baby is born, every day when true love happens in any shape or form. It is spectacularly revealed in the miracle of forgiveness, or wherever bridges are built to replace walls. And, lest we forget the astonishment of it all, (and forgetfulness is our abiding darkness) we often sit with friends around a Sunday table, and recognise and remember the Love Story in the breaking of bread. And we are happy, because we know for sure, through all our long nights and cold winters, our sins, our wars, our madness, that it is the same incarnate, eternal light and love that is slowly drawing everything and everybody Home.

Pope Francis keeps reminding us that the first momentous nanosecond of Creation is already the beginning of a special story about God, a precious book in which every page, every creature, is a self-revelation of a divine Creator. He is saying that God was already in the world from the beginning of its existence, long before the coming of Jesus into our world at the first Christmas comparatively recently. He believes that Creation itself is a central part of the Christian story; that Evolution is the first (and continuing) love letter from our Parent-God, the Risen Christ, the Holy Spirit; and that Creation, Evolution, Incarnation, Eucharist blend together in the most beautiful way as beacons that light our way into the heart and home of God; and that our God indeed, is astonishingly human!

❦ 66 ❦

'TEARS OF THINGS'

I cried a lot those late summer days. It may have been due to old age. Today David Attenborough has admitted to crying more than ever before: the most recent reason being the plight of the young penguins dying in the Antarctic. Apart from being my first reaction to the news and fear of cancer I'm not sure why I cry now. But that response has spread out into other vulnerable dimensions of my life, as though the possibility of losing it soon has opened up a heightened sensitivity to deeper things. A lone seagull swooping across my window can do it. Or a giggling child on her father's back. Or the first browning of the leaves. Memories of my mother, of Christmas, of my own experiences. I cry at things of pathos, of beauty, of cruelty, of terror. Sometimes it's more an emotional prayer for those who are marked out for another long day of torture. Mothers who are waking up to their first day, utterly destroyed and longing to die, without their beloved child or husband. There's been a huge increase in those magic moments when some experience of the senses sends me whirling back to childhood - a stream in a flat field, a tiny tot trying to climb aboard the patient family dog, the lit windows of a house in the distance. Certain words of intimacy in an email, a touch I know that's full of compassion, the look of love, a lush, descending strain of a Mozart concerto. Above all, almost any photo of my brother Joseph, who had Down's syndrome.

Shortly before his execution for the part he played in the Irish Easter Rising of 1916, I'm sure that mystic-soldier Padraig Pearse was weeping when he wrote his poignant *The Wayfarer*:

The beauty of the world hath made me sad,
This beauty that will pass;
Sometimes my heart hath shaken with great joy
To see a leaping squirrel in a tree,
Or a red lady-bird upon a stalk,
Or little rabbits in a field at evening,
Lit by a slanting sun...
Or children with bare feet upon the sands
Of some ebbed sea, or playing on the streets
Of little towns in Connacht;
Things young and happy.
And then my heart hath told me:
These will pass,
Will pass and change, will die and be no more,
Things bright and green, things young and happy;
And I have gone upon my way
Sorrowful.[48]

I will cry a lot more – of this I'm sure – at our inability to live in, even to notice the wonder of Creation; to be caught up in the graced mystery of Evolution; in the astonishing transformation of going to Mass; in the touch and smell of God in every relationship; in her delight in dancing the cosmos into its expansion; in the divine artistry, humour, surprise and transformation in every single moment that happens; and, even as the Pope assured us, "in every speck of dust in nature". They are not all tears of doom and gloom, of desperation, despair and sadness. Neither are they tears of hilarity, success or victory. They are the 'tears of things', the *lacrima rerum*, that lie at the heart of everything.

I cry at my own ignorance, my failure to fall in love with God through her Creation, her sheer humanity, her exciting divinity: all finally revealed in the one human being Jesus; and then in every human being and in every created entity. The contemplation of mystery, of the silhouetted end barely glimpsed, is a source of joy, astonishment, wonder, contentment and healing... It is also behind many tears. A significant part of this kind of meditation is a willingness to let go of what we thought we knew in order to touch on truths of which we never dreamed. We must unlearn a great many weird doctrines before we can move on to the original vision, insight and meaning we were born to find: that we ourselves *are* the Temple (1 Cor 3: 16) that God dwells in us, chooses to dwell inside creation (1 Tim 6: 16). God is the essence and being and centre at the heart of every tear of life and every smile of delight. Swimming and floating in God, we are rivers of living water, tears and joy, flowing from the oceans of divinity at our deepest core. Such thoughts, words, insights bring temporary slants of light through the cracks in my darkness.

67

LOVE BEFORE KNOWLEDGE

We are now at the beginning of October. I have always celebrated this week when we honour those special saints Thérèse and Francis of Assisi. They specialised in living the way of unconditional love. They knew spiritual things, as St Paul put it, "in a spiritual way". With Teilhard de Chardin, they regarded love as the most universal, the most tremendous and the most mysterious personal and cosmic force. Teilhard's wish was that humanity would perceive the reality of the universe, and that of every human soul, shining in the spirit and through the flesh. Carlo Carretto tries to find examples of pure love. "When a parent gazes into the eyes of their child, they will, if they look carefully, see the mystery of the infinite, of the unfathomable, of the ungraspable. For an instant we have shared in God's creative joy, we have touched the infinite."[49] So much divine unconditional love in the eyes of a small child!

The life and love of the human heart is not about knowledge. "Information is not transformation," Thomas Merton reminds us. It took years to understand this, wrote Richard Rohr, that love precedes knowledge. During these long nights as I struggle with the ultimate meaning of my inner demons and outer diminishments, of my failure to understand God's presence in what is happening to me, I'm sure that what I seek is beyond thought, reason and intelligence. It is found, I'm discovering, and only vaguely, in another place. "For now we see in a mirror dimly, but then we shall see face to face. Now I know only in part; then I will know fully, just as I have been fully known myself." (1 Cor 13: 12)

When the saints say that we belong to God by way of participation rather than knowledge or religious behaviour, by experience rather than obedience, I try to see my dark and bright situations, my shocking upset, in terms of God's own light and darkness. Through it all I remembered the words of Sufi teacher Hazrat Inayat Khan, "God is Love, Lover and Beloved". Most Western mystics *exemplified* contemplation, as did Jesus, much more than they directly spoke about it. It is caught rather than taught. Many Catholic Christians have long forgotten this fundamental truth, and that is why reclaiming good theology and its practice is now so important. And so I turn to meditation or contemplation as my saviour, my true vision, my sacramental second-sight. It is where all the deepest differences and paradoxes, where thinking and feeling are held together.

As I awake to another troubled day I remember that great suffering and great love can nourish within us the same mind, which is in 'Christ Jesus' (Phil 2: 5-11). In fact Rohr would say that at this moment, the incarnate Christ himself is thinking in us, through us - and *as* us. It is because Incarnation means that now the essence of God is revealed in our humanity, the divine heart beating in time and tune in our human one, the true face of God in our very deepest selves. Because the revelation of Incarnation is of an indwelling God, the core of our deepest self, we often fail to recognise God's loving and intimate presence precisely because the Mystery is living so close to us. We are still looking for a non-existent God 'out there'.

Faith in God is not just about believing in doctrines or spiritual ideas. It is to have confidence in love itself, in reality itself, in what actually happens to us as the evolution of life unfolds, bringing intolerable pain and much joy. This is the meaning of the Incarnation according to Rohr. God is in everything, revealed in all things even through the tragic and sad, as the revolutionary doctrine of the cross reveals. I spend so much time these long days trying to figure out whether I should pray for the lifting of this cross from my shoulders, or pray to accept what life brings, which is the unfolding of God's evolving and loving plan for me. What *is*, is love, so much so that even my current experience of fear, loss, death is being used for purposes of transformation into love. How then can I pray to God to have all of this grace-bearing experience of the cross miraculously removed from me when it is God's own unfolding self that brings this heavily disguised gift of salvation? Created as we are in God's image, who and what we truly are is love, each of us revealing it in our own particular way; in cancer and in health.

68

MORNINGS

Mornings are not the symbol of light, beginnings and hope for everyone. I'm at my lowest in the morning. It's when everything seems daunting. It's when the worst possible interpretation of things fills my mind. I've tried many strategies, searched for many resources, practised all kinds of remedies. Nothing lasts for long. Especially now that my health prognosis is even more serious than at first suspected. My mind is so vulnerable during those small hours, a victim of the demons of negativity and fear. Barely awake, they have already arrived and settled in. And like a rabbit in the dazzling light of the coming threat, my mind seems utterly powerless to defend itself.

One simple way to deal with this is to get up immediately, make a cuppa tea, try a few minutes of contemplative prayer to come to terms with this destructive tumour that is throwing a cold new light on everything and that is radically diminishing all aspects of my present and future existence on this planet. Yet this seems so impossible to do when caught in that invisible web of self-absorption and self-pity. I force myself to repeat some tried and trusted verses and sentences that seem to 'work' during the day, often to no avail. I try everything and anything that will distract me from despair, make another liveable day possible, trust a little more, stretch my faith to cover each new bit of alarming possibilities up ahead.

There are times when I get some help from the sentiments and phrases I generally practise each morning but with the added urgency of the changed horizon of my life, the ever-present coping with the severities of the chemo side-effects, and the anxiety I feel about the whole stoma experience. I try to console myself with the belief that I *can* do much to lessen the darkness of each coming day by the way

I think about it. And every morning I have a choice. I cannot escape the many pains of cancer but I have a choice around how I handle it. Suffering itself is a fact; *how I see it is a choice*. I can change my destiny and how I prepare for it by changing my attitude to it. I return regularly now to ponder some of these positive thoughts and clarifying truths about the grace of choice that I put together in *The Healing Habit* a few years ago.

In that wee book I remind myself that being caught in this web of pain, which has suddenly tangled up and twisted my intense plans for my life, places me where the real dawn of a new perspective, a new way of seeing and being, a higher and deeper level of courage, can emerge from this dim mental mess within me in the here and now. Maybe this is what is meant by seeing pain as the teacher within, and suffering as the surprising, unexpected, hidden gift (*The Healing Habit*, p 46). Another effort to make the morning less depressing is to remember something that the Persian mystic Rumi wrote: "Get up early. The breezes at dawn have secrets to tell you. Do not go back to sleep; do not go back to sleep."

Currently, these mornings of my melancholic mind seem to be trying to indicate something. That is my need to surrender more absolutely to the cancer which is spreading, not shrinking. Anything else is doomed to failure and depression. None of those helpful kinds of positive thinking, of strategies, resources and remedies (above) are the perfect answer. There are none. Only further trust. There seems to be a quiet insistent call to another place, to a deeper silence, beyond any kind of mind control or God-control. There is no external God 'out there', as we keep insisting, to be influenced or persuaded by anything we can think, do or say. The kind of love we are called to/called for lies beyond all we consider spiritual or righteous. In the face of the ultimate and utter falling in love which is all Jesus wants of us, labels like 'holy', 'religious', 'conservative' or 'liberal' are like straw in a storm, utterly unrelated to the tender and wholehearted submission to the piercing eyes of a tremendous lover. "Forget all you know," writes the author of *The Cloud of*

Unknowing. "Begin with the heart" we remember from the twelfth century mystic Meister Eckhart.

Daily I notice how shallow my breathing has become. Many times a day I pause to find its natural rhythm again. This simple exercise has an immediate balancing and grounding effect. There is no part of us that is not affected and restored by our natural awareness of our breathing. There is no end to the stream of books available that testify to the central part played by our breathing in the calming, grounding and healing of our souls and bodies. It is mainly about building the habit of awareness of the deliberate rhythm of the body's natural timing. Even before I get out of bed each day, this may bring a momentary release from the blind anxiety, from those negative and draining places, and one step further away from the hovering threat of panic. God's calming grace already lives in my darkest places; what is missing is my awareness of that ever-present gift.

Another thought helps me too. I try to instil it into my brain before it is hijacked by the demons of negativity. Spiritual teacher Eckhart Tolle reminds us that we see things, not as *they* are (maybe harmless, neutral, objective, neither threatening nor critical), but as *we* are (fearful, fragile, victimised, worried, seeing the worst outcome not the best, vulnerable). This insight has often been a blessing in my struggle with the morning demons.

Now we often have to be satisfied with these and other temporary remedies. They can all help to save us, and become part of a greater redemption. But they are not the full story, or the complete answer, for no religion, no culture, no book, no person is. They may be good guides, useful wrappings, maps, pointers towards the sublime Mystery, towards the final surrender. But the incarnate soul of God and humanity lie and intertwine at the point of great suffering and great love. We have read this before in these pages. We have, in fact, read far more than we need in order to find God's golden thread. We read more, make more pilgrimages, follow more devotions to favourite saints, attend more spiritual retreats and courses – and all of these practices, rituals and outward activities are often necessary and most helpful – but they are not enough. They are the beginning but we think they are the end, the podium of success rather than the beginning of a long learning. They are the map rather than the destiny and there comes a time when the whisper of deep truth, the faint grace notes of a new melody must reach our innermost being, when a new light reveals the seduction of shortcuts and instant cures.

From the story of the Incarnation we gather that everything created reveals the fleshed presence of God without any exception: our planet, our bodies, our experiences and yes, my cancer. Because my tumour reveals a face of God too it is not 'the enemy' or a divine test or trial from God to be hated. A true interpretation of the mystery of Incarnation (an interpretation that seems to have eluded the mainstream churches in the most alarming and shocking way) would see no tension or dualistic separation between anything earthly and anything heavenly, anything sacred and anything secular.

In contemplation I try to see that God's creation of evolution, of development by the life/death sequence is in every single aspect of nature: everything has to follow this pattern. My cancer, the diminishment of my life, the fact maybe of an imminent death, *has to happen.* There is no 'pick and choose', no changing of an interfering God by the power of our prayers and devotions: there is only the presence or absence of our ability to surrender to the inevitable will of God in our lives, our alignment with Creation, Evolution and the death and life sequence with Him who never cursed his terrible death on a cross but 'freely accepted' it, as every Eucharistic Prayer insists.

But right now do I believe this? Do I wake up every wretched morning protected from my depression and despair? Do I? No. Incarnation is not an instant result, a magic wand. We begin by exploring the meaning of Incarnation working through our human weakness and doubts. So I ask myself if these months of necessary suffering are really redemptive or not. Is this the time for me to endure another most deadly cradling? Where are the glimpses of the love I write of in this current 'calvary'? Six months ago, before the bad news arrived, I could have answered such questions in countlessly clever ways.

But no more. No more answers, explanations, learned insights into God's plans, some of which, I'm afraid may have crept onto these very pages. For want of any other response I can only conclude that it has something to do with love.

From the harsh mess that now surrounds me, I try to put some invisible shape to it. Love, only love. Blind love. Lost-in-the-dark love. Faith love, inexplicable, mysterious and utterly free love. My effort to live this love in my heart is the real and deepest truth about me now. Only there am I in the true force field of love. Only there can I suffer my cancer as a hidden life-force rather than a fearful, stress-filled death-energy.

And every now and then, before my faith completely evaporates, before I fall again into despair, before the dark gets impossibly unbearable, and life gets unliveable, a crumb of bread and a sip of wine are given to me to remind me of what we always were, always are, and no matter what, always will be – love.

❦ 69 ❦

NO OTHER WAY

My contemplation today, if you could call it that, is about allowing myself and my pain, for a moment in the course of this winter season of my life, to be shaped and fashioned into the point where the *image* of God in which I was born, and the *likeness* of God toward which we struggle to aspire, meet. It is the embrace for which I was created, and now, on a good day, I want to surrender to it, trust it, willing it to happen in this definitive new interior life that I must nourish and depend on with all my heart. To reach this point, even in the most elementary way, is already an invisible explosion and gift of grace. (This image is at the heart of Eastern spirituality; in baptism the image of God is revealed, and during the course of our lives we strive to transform that image into the very divine likeness here and now on this earth. Russian Orthodox Metropolitan Anthony wrote of the point where God's image and likeness coincide, "the stage we have already reached, perhaps only momentarily, fleetingly, in becoming what we are called to be".)

Richard Rohr puts it another way. He asks us to see our wounds (my inoperable cancer) as *the way through*, as Jesus did. Then they become sacred wounds rather than scars to deny, disguise or project onto others. This frightening threat of a suddenly shortened life is really not an obstacle, he is saying, it is a gift! Even though you, the reader, may have noticed that this has been my horizon from the beginning of this book, you may also have noticed how little 'progress' I've made. Inner healing and acceptance of our pain is indeed a very long journey. And if we do not try with all our energy, day by day, minute by minute to keep moving in that direction, then we become cynical, negative or, worst of all, bitter. And this negative diminishment of the spirit within us will be dumped on those close to us; those who personally care for us, our family and friends. Many of us will remember the truest words: "If we do not transform our pain, we will most assuredly transmit it."

For many of our spiritual writers, the key to achieving this inner transformation is to search for the divine love and meaning in our suffering. What can possibly be the significance of my cancer and its terrible destruction? Where on earth can I find God in my suffering? During these very days of my despair can I find anything positive or strengthening to sustain me? In his desire to support us Rohr reminds us that we should not try to get rid of our pain until we've learned what it has to teach. What good can it do for myself or for others? He refers to that 'liminal space' in which we can hold our pain consciously and trustfully. Here we are open to learning and breaking through to a much deeper level of faith and mystery. On most days I am not open to such a possibility; tearfully, I remain closed.

"We must all carry the cross of our own reality," Rohr writes, "until God transforms us through it." That is one way to become 'a wounded healer', one who has fully faced her own wounds and in doing that can heal others. But how can I absorb my pain so it becomes a grace, hold my suffering until it becomes redemptive for myself and others, accept this premature warning of my death so it becomes the energy of resurrection for me and for the world? In my heyday I believed and spoke rather glibly and confidently in such fine terms. May I repeat here what I wrote in the introduction: I do not for a moment doubt the utter Christian truth of such spiritual searchings, but I had little understanding of the actual torture of experiencing, enduring, the dark nights and days that are happening to me now. Until this happens, I'm told, such a transformation will never be a reality, and will never infuse a deeper wisdom into my shallow spirituality. But I must remember also that there is a huge danger in trying too hard to feel or understand anything much about the inscrutable ways, mind and heart of our beautiful Mother-God. At the end of our exploring we will still have to trust, to surrender, to accept, and to be more aware of the mystery.

"That is why," according to Rohr, "Jesus praises a certain quality even more than love, and he calls it *faith*. It is the ability to stand in liminal space, to stand on the threshold, to hold the contraries, until we are moved by grace to a much deeper level and a much larger frame, where our private pain is not centre stage but a mystery shared with every act of bloodshed and every tear wept since the beginning of time. Our pain is not just our own."[50]

70

THE WOUND - THE TEACHER
WITHIN

In common with suffering, thoughtful millions who, in a warring world of evil and destruction, doubt and wonder about the meaning of a saving God, I too have hard questions now. Can people walk through a children's hospital ward and still believe in a loving Saviour? David Attenborough asks many questions about a God who will not, or cannot remove the worm that is eating into the baby's eye. There are massive questions about innocent suffering. There are times when I sit down, breathe deeply, and when dark thoughts close in, try to remember anything that might help me understand something of the mystery of these huge human issues; things that I can use for comfort, support, courage, meaning, for seeing my way through the presence of intense suffering, of rampant evil, of the triumph of the anti-Christ.

In his book *When Bad Things Happen to Good People* Rabbi Harold Kushner reflects on these issues too. How can there be a good or just God in a world wracked with pain, how can we call God a loving Mother in the face of so much wanton destruction? What is the point of praying to such a cold and callous operator? Again, there are no easy answers. For everything we hold about our unbidden suffering, there is a contrary viewpoint too.

Susan Sontag in her *Letter to Borges* offers an optimistic vision of the wound as a mysterious resource. All our experiences – even the most negative and humiliating – are, in her view, material given to us as raw material from which we may fashion our work and future. In her *An Interrupted Life* Etty Hillesum, a young Jewish woman who died at *Auschwitz*, wrote: "It still all comes down to the same thing: life is beautiful. And I believe in God. And I want to be there right in the thick of what people call *horror* and still be able to say: life is beautiful."[51]

Sooner or later coping with suffering becomes central to our lives. Some of the greatest wisdom has come from those who are no strangers to pain themselves. People who suffer a lot are always seeking some kind of meaning in what they go through. *Man's Search for Meaning* was written by Viktor Frankl who, as a Holocaust survivor, suffered so deeply for so long without becoming embittered or despairing. Finding meaning in his terrible condition became the pursuit of his life of pain. We give meaning to our suffering by the way we reflect on and respond to it. In itself it is meaningless. Frankl realised that life's hard ways can take away everything you possess except one thing: your freedom to choose how you respond to your circumstances and wounds and 'enemies'.

He kept himself sane and humanly authentic and free by protecting, nourishing and practising this priceless grace, in spite of his persecutors' redoubled efforts to break his will and his soul. He cherished his graced ability to forgive them for their endless gratuitous cruelty at every moment of every day even though they fiercely tried to make him hate their very guts. In my own current circumstances at this hour of my life, it might mean that while I cannot control the power of my cancer in any way, I can control my reaction to it, my response to it; how I receive it, live with it, think and feel, and what I do about it. I find immense and helpful wisdom in the reflections of people like Frankl who have suffered beyond description, and yet, in and only through that suffering, have found an invincible light to sustain them for life.

For Etty Hillesum, it was the significance of her suffering that kept her relentlessly free within herself. Her struggle in the madness and evil of the concentration camps was both deeply and despairingly human and utterly divine. "We seek the meaning of life," she wrote in her journals, "wondering whether any meaning can be left ... perhaps life has its own meaning, even if it takes a lifetime to find it... for a moment yesterday I felt I was about to collapse under a tremendous weight... I feel like a small battlefield in which some of the problems of our time are being fought out – to allow oneself to be a battlefield."[52] Commenting on these words, Richard Rohr said this is what it means to hold together the contradictions and pain of the world, of humanity, of each one, without despair.

❦ 71 ❦

FACES OF SUFFERING

We are called to be both the agony and ecstasy of God for the health and wellbeing of the world; to accept and to somehow participate in the mystery of death and resurrection deep in one's own soul and in the life of the universe. Reading and trying to interiorise some of these wise reflections brings healing for someone like me just now. That is, on those occasions when they break through the negative thoughts that seem to be my current default mode. They attach, reveal and unfold a hugely significant reason and meaning in what might too often be received and regarded as an arbitrary, useless and evil visitation.

My sense of somehow belonging to the Earth, of being the child of the Great Spirit, of carrying a responsibility for the health of a universe that is the body of God, affects me now in unexpected ways. Somehow I am responsible to everyone for everything, as Fyodor Dostoyevsky put it. For all of this to be happening to me I must try to understand so much more about the fragility, vulnerability and ambiguity of our evolving world. Social psychologist Diarmuid O'Murchu takes us deeper into the mystery when he writes that "creation cannot survive, and less so thrive, without its dark side. There is a quality of destruction, decay and death that is essential to creation's flourishing... And the consequence of this destructive dimension is what we call evil, pain and suffering."[53] And it is all paradox writ large. We must first come to terms with the unfolding cycle of birth-death-rebirth, which is patterned all over creation from the tiniest atom to the expanding cosmos.

In recent decades, I've become aware, you may have noticed, that in any meditation or contemplation about God (or whatever name you may wish to use for the Great Spirit of Life, the Mystery of Being, our

Eternal Lover), the whole New Universe Story, the daily discoveries of physicists and scientists, the revelations of the central place played by Evolution, have to be at the centre of all our musings. It will take time, but already our theologians and spiritual writers are so excited at the way our understanding of God and Creation is being transformed by these new, powerful, mysterious scientific revelations. In my current daily temptations to give in to despairing tears, I continue to find light and lift in this vague understanding of my perceived and necessary participation in the rising-dying-rising of an evolving world. My suffering plays a central part in the evolving of our broken earth and of my own broken evolving body; both bodies being the precious, the beloved and the one, broken body of God.

Something else struck me a few days ago. I never once believed that God in any way sends us anything but true and good life, as pain-free and abundant as can be. Saddled with the image of an all-powerful, all-knowing, controlling, male God we had no way of dealing with the reality of suffering except by pushing some highly damaging devotional teaching about God sending us crosses during our lives to test us, to teach us a lesson, to purify us from original sin, to show us who's boss. Because of my certainty regarding my own fallible mother's love for me, I never understood how the most loving 'Person' ever, could deliberately allow pain or even inflict torture on young and old, to examine and check out our love for our Creator. Imagine your mother sticking pins into you when you were small just to make sure that you loved her!

In spite of all the reflections in this section about the grace hidden within suffering, there persists a poisonous indoctrination that needs repeated reassurance for God's (all) people that suffering is never a punishment for sin. This terrible and destructive spiritual teaching has destroyed a key element of the Christian faith. Again, as we have already touched on and arising from a thoroughly flawed doctrine of original sin, we have believed that God literally and historically turfed a non-existent Adam and Eve out of a non-existent garden, having been seduced by a non-existent, multilingual snake. When our

Church's theological clean-up takes place we will be horrified at how gullible and naïve we all have been in believing such love-destroying fallacies. (Please check out the beautiful meaning of the Adam and Eve myth, with its revelation about humanity's attraction to what is dark and evil; but also humanity's openness to the bright light of divinity that will always outshine the deadly shadows that also live within us.) The deadly theory of making daily and lifelong reparation to a very dissatisfied and angry God because of our 'first parents' original sin' has never entered my thoughts about my current situation. I beg of you, dear reader, please, in the name of a love that is sublime, supreme and so intimate, that is as tender and passionate and personal as you have ever encountered, do not let those destructive thoughts, even for one second, ever influence your heart.

⚜ 72 ⚜

A SUFFERING GOD

Another simplistic explanation for the baffling question of the seem-ingly random tragedies and accidents happening to children and innocent people, has been the notion that in this life we look at the tapestry of our lives from the back, full of incomprehensible criss-crosses of thread and fabric, but when we get to heaven all will be revealed when we see the brilliant front of it. While still small, I remember thinking, 'Tell that to the mother of the baby who is dying of child-cancer.' But we never said a word, did we? Already brain-washed and fearful, we just carried on trying to love this Creator who continually allows, and even plans, the terrible pains of the most innocent and purest of creatures. And these destructive teachings are still taught, and many still try to believe them. Most people now though, unable to believe these untruths and unafraid of ecclesiastical condemnation, simply walk away. And who can blame them?

There is a belief that God sends us the burden of pain because we are strong enough to handle it. But why? To prove what? How did we (and our parents) believe such empty and false explanations? Think again of a mother or father. This is never the loving way – the 'tough love' of God that many fathers offered as a pretext for the abuse of their families. But God never sends anything but love. It is life itself that brings us to the pain and the problems. It is fate, simply, that I am participating in the darkness of those of us diagnosed with cancer. God is as devastated as I am, weeps as some of my friends do, would die again to avoid the slightest cry of pain from any of us. We just happen to be living in an evolving world with its necessary break-downs and breakthroughs. We may not want to believe it, but we are forever an indispensable dimension of all of nature. We have touched on this already. I know it's a lot to reflect on, but once our Mother-God surrendered herself to Incarnation in Jesus, even she could not avoid being caught up in the time and space-bound, unfolding and developing of Creation, of life, of incarnate love.

Richard Rohr writes: "I believe – if I am to believe Jesus – that God *is* suffering love. If we are created in God's image, and if there is so much suffering in the world, then God must also *be* suffering. How else can we understand the revelation of the cross? Why else would the central Christian logo be a naked, bleeding, suffering divine-human wretch?" It took us priests long enough to realise one of the many forgotten central truths of Incarnation, and we still don't – that Jesus is not merely observing the pain and wounds of human beings from a distance (heaven?); rather is he somehow at the centre of human suffering, with us, for us, through us and *as* us. Our own individual suffering is somehow at the heart of the co-redemption of the world as "all creation groans in one great act of giving birth" (Rom 8: 22). My growing conviction these days is that my cancer plays a big part in "making up in my own body all that still has to be undergone for the sake of the Whole Body of God" (Col 1: 24).

In my state of loss, this evening, before I go to bed early, I comfort myself with this prayer from God to me, 'I know the pain you are going through, the knife of wounds that cut you open. Don't run away. Learn from this experience, as I did. Hang there for a while as I did. It will be your teacher. Rather than long life now you will be gaining a larger life soon. It is not the end, it is the way through. For you, there is no choice because I'm holding you so closely. For you, it is the only way. Give it everything like I did.' It helps so much to recognise our suffering is not our own, it is not only about me. It helps us realise that we are actually living inside a larger force-field of life and death: when I can see and accept my suffering as part of the wounds of my life, of humanity's life, of the life of Jesus, of cosmic life, of the incarnate life of the living God. Only then, the wise ones say, can we begin to understand Incarnation and actually experience salvation. It is the power, the stubbornness, the intense vanity of the ego that forever constitutes the greatest blockage. It is so hard to learn that, according to Rohr, "suffering is the only thing strong enough to destabilise the imperial ego".

❧ 73 ❧

MOMENT OF TRUTH

November winds carry echoes of loss. And of beyond. It is the month when memories and absences haunt our hearts, when the saint and the sinner converse in our soul, when the universe itself seems to sense the sad season of a perennial ending and beginning. We are learning that belonging and the great pain of loss go together. We must let go so as to find, and become. If you love you are sure to suffer; if you do not love you will suffer even more. Great love and great suffering will always be the threshold of mystery.

I'm writing this on the 9th day of November 2018. It is a day, for me, that is heavy with love, loss and courage, fitting for an autumnal setting. The most important day in my life was 82 years ago when I slid into planet Earth. In a sense, yesterday comes next in importance: because yesterday we made a momentous decision to begin the slow slide out of it again. A chat with the consultant revealed that the first course of chemo (including the use of a particularly severe drug called *cetuximab*) had been ineffective and would be discontinued. Also, a CT scan showed that my initial bowel cancer had spread to the liver, lungs and the peritoneum, making it now inoperable and incurable; thus presenting a stark picture to those doing all they could to help, to heal, to enhance, to pray for the quality of my life into the future.

For as long as I have left to live I will never forget that conversation when, with my brother Micheál and *anam cara* Margaret, I weighed up the guidance of the consultants about the pros and cons of the situation, and then decided to surrender to the stuttering flow of life without chemotherapy, to a future sustained in alignment with the growing of my tumour, enfolded in grace, and the evolving of my precious world, inside and out. I'm not sure why, but this poem brought me a certain confidence:

> *You feel that dangers hold you tight*
> *Remember, nature guards you well.*
> *The way you are is shield all right*
> *From horrors heaped up out of sight.*
> *Be sure that nature guards you well;*
> *Trembling within, without so bright,*
> *Don't doubt there was a saving spell*
> *Cast at your birth for your delight;*
> *Your very nature guards you well.*[54]

I woke with a start this morning. And immediately asked myself what in God's name did we decide on yesterday? I'm asking myself the question at this precise, vulnerable and startling moment. In deciding, with professional understanding, to forego all chemo treatment, to accept the fact that there will be no healing, curing or even mitigating of the tumour's growth, I have opted for a long, or short lifespan, over which I have no control. Rohr, you will remember, defined suffering as the experience of being out of control, of having no power to help ourselves, about the moment we have to surrender our existence, our lives, our experiences, our future, into the hands of another. This is a first for me. Being a priest, there are resources, support, financial security often denied to others. In the West, most Roman Catholic priests will not want for the best of medication, care, accommodation and surgery. We can usually find a way. But not always! And so, when the chips are down and the future is bleak, and we have run out of cures and solutions, even priests who are really religious, very holy indeed, may lack the spiritual depth to cushion cancer.

And the day comes, in one way or another for each one, when the pros and cons of our lives are weighed up, when the balance has changed, and we know, like Jesus did, that it's time to go. For as long as I have left, can I willingly stay convinced of this elusive truth: "For now we see in a mirror dimly but then we shall see God face to face. Now I know only in part; then I will know fully just as I have been fully known myself"? (1 Cor 13: 12) In the meantime, I will search for meaning and love wherever I can sense these saving graces. My life, I tell myself, has not lost its meaning. Something in our soul forever senses possibility. In *Love without Frontiers*, poet Phoebe Hesketh wrote:

> *A love without frontiers that sees without eyes,*
> *Is present in absence and never denies*
> *The unexplored country beyond.*[55]

Again I ask what yesterday's shocking decision is telling me? Many things, I want to believe, things I could never have vaguely and yet deeply glimpsed without this other death. One of these glimpses is around the sublime, unimaginable nature of being unconditionally loved. God, I sense, can be loved but not figured out; experienced but not thought through; embraced but not by thinking; felt but not through rational analysis; surrendered to but not through willpower. In my searching for even a temporary relief from my current growing fear of an impending season of death's pain, I'm finding through contemplation, that my study, my head-knowledge, my rational, logical reasoning are not helping at all. It is more a case of knowing through union with a person, whereby we can enjoy an intuitive grasp of wholeness, a truth beyond words, beyond any need to convince others or prove anything right or wrong.

❧ 74 ❧

A NEW EARTH...

(What now follows, for the remainder of the book, are a few thoughts, insights, convictions and glimpses that are occurring to me in the aftermath of that recent and momentous decision that I must live with and die with. In light of my current circumstances please try to understand that the reflections, as recorded here, are not always sequential, logical or coherent!)

Stephen Hawking, just before his death, said that there is no God and no afterlife – it is but wishful thinking. We can all believe whatever we want. When we die we return to dust. This had been his growing conviction for some time. It came to light again recently on the occasion of the launching of *Brief Answers to the Big Questions*, a project he had begun not long before his death in March 2018. But notice what he has also written or said on numerous occasions. This is my summary of them and I want to comment on them in a moment: "Remember to look up at the stars, not down at your feet. Try to make sense of what you see. Wonder about what makes the universe exist. Be curious and remember, however difficult life may be, there is always something you can do and succeed at. It matters that you do not give up. Unleash imagination. Shape the future. The future for young people will depend more on science and technology than on religion."

I often try to figure out how so many of our most intelligent scholars (e.g. Stephen Hawking, Richard Dawkins, Christopher Hitchens et al) seem to have failed, like so many Christians I'm afraid, to 'get' the shocking and most astonishing meaning of Incarnation. They think all Catholics still believe in a distant God 'out there', a God with favourites whose prayers God 'answers' and others from whom he turns away his face; that our faith seems to be an amalgamation of superstition, mysterious devotions, and unformed theology and spirituality. It seems beyond them to accept that many Catholic Christians ponder a God within, whose very love-energy sets our hearts alive and alight with a divine/human intimacy and creativity; a God whose very essence is the same love-energy that exploded in the Big Bang and is the sustaining element within the Evolution of Creation that scientists are discovering, with excitement and wonder, every new day in our own time as never before.

Yet look again at the words Stephen Hawking used, and try to see them as the imagination and presence of the incarnate God's self-expression in our beautiful, beloved and broken planet – curiosity, wonder, imagination, gazing at the stars – all words and phrases, as you know, I'm forever using to hint at the very essence and nature of the incarnate God of the Christians. Nor do these brilliant scientists and students of life seem to accept that humanity is forever needed to facilitate the salvation and completion of the earth, transforming it into heaven. They will have no truck with such an interpretation of Incarnation. No one is asking them to *believe* these truly Catholic Christian revelations, but to accept that our faith can complement their own precious work and world-view. Why, dear reader, am I bombarding you with these thoughts and ideas? Only because they make such a difference to me in the way I'm now beginning to cope with the rest of my new life. You will remember the comfort, peace and healing brought to my restless soul by the drops of divine wisdom that percolate into my being these nights.

❦ 75 ❦

...AND A NEW HEAVEN

Nor have these scientists any time for an afterlife. This question too is much on my mind these days as the time of my death has lurched forwards startlingly and significantly. Please have patience with me as I try to express why I have recently been so excited and captivated by, and fallen in love with the possibilities around one of God's many astonishing secrets. May I begin the story this way? Just think of the chrysalis before it morphs into a stunning butterfly, the seed before it begins to find its feet of oak, the foetus before it leaves the womb for an utterly different and glorious way of existing. As they grow and develop in ways beyond their initial comprehension, they all have sublime moments of awe and unsuspected, unexpected transformation. They could never have even dreamt of such possibilities. Imagine a conversation between unborn twins. One sees absolutely no way of believing in any form of existence outside the womb. How could there be? Everything that has meaning for him, that sustains him, that inspires and completes him, is present only where he now lives. For some sublime reason the other is not so certain! She leaves room for mystery, for the power of love, for a blessed imagination. And yet, pragmatically, and as though there never was an Incarnation, many of us believe, like the first baby, that leaving the womb of this world is the end of us, too.

Now that the matter is more, for me, than a mere theological point, since we're talking here about my impending death and afterlife, I keep reflecting on reasons for the existence of a heaven: utterly beyond my understanding of course, but just as an exciting possibility. Think of the most spectacular achievements and creations that have impressed you; think of the countless wonders of the world and of its inhabitants; reflect on the deepest, indescribable experiences of beauty, pathos and intensity; think of the intensely moving emotions found in novels, films, paintings, dance, poetry, nature herself: all of these belong to this earthly dispensation.

Come the next evolutionary breakthrough, both personal when we die and cosmic when the sun burns out in billions of years' time, there will be another world surpassing this most beautiful planet and cosmos, another existence and a new way of being for creation and humanity. Surpassing all imagination, beyond our dreams and experiences, the Bible assures us, we move on to grow anew, from the womb of another place, bringing with us the best of ourselves, the highest and most sublime moments of our time here, our truest relationships and timeless dreams. "Eye has not seen, nor ear heard, neither has it entered into the heart of man to conceive, what God has prepared for those who love him." (1 Cor 2: 9)

And will the next world be a continuation of this earth, a place of discovery and development, a place of peaceful communities? When will we begin to see this world through entirely transformed eyes and with a heart that truly believes the main and stunning revelation of Incarnation: that everything and everyone is both divine and eternal? Everything, because it is a reflection, a dimension, a presence of God, will last forever. There's too much love and beauty around to let us slip out of sight forever after the briefest few years on Planet Earth. Of this I'm sure – my upcoming death will not be the end of me. I bet my (next) life on it!

May I try again? After all, we are truly travelling in the land of mystery here. Just reflect on the billion stages and breakthroughs of evolution; some small, some universal and some cosmic. These have been happening since the beginning of time. And in the bigger picture, this will continue for billions of years to come. We live in a universe that is evolving towards final fulfilment, towards the horizons of Omega, when 'God is all in all'. Just as the baby must think that leaving the womb is the end of its world, so with us. So often our agnostic temptations are but the failure of imagination. Our smartest people, as we have just seen, cannot countenance the existence of a heaven. After decades of doubt I now cannot wait for this moment: yes, to weep at death for the loss of our most enchanting and sacred world (despite its inexplicable ugliness, madness and evil) but also to carry a deep 'curiosity' (the word used by Hawking earlier), a loving anticipation of the warmest welcome by our unconditionally-loving Artist-God.

Imagination and Evolution. There is little doubt about the graced breakthroughs of evolution already, gradually growing us into who we are in our lives right now, and who we will one day actually become. (And it isn't just all about us. For all we know there may be billions of life-cherishing planets that have completed this divinely epic journey, or are, like us, just beginning that long, beautiful and daunting, evolving road.) We know and believe these astonishing happenings as the imagination of our Creator, the work of the Holy Spirit. In his *The Universe is a Green Dragon* physicist Brian Swimme writes: "Four billion years ago planet Earth was molten rock: now it sings opera . . . the universe shivers with wonder in the depths of the human."[56] Countless Christian scientists see these astonishing truths as the self-revelation of a Gracious God, the artistry of her hands. And many others just wonder at the unfolding and beautiful mystery.

Incarnation impels us to believe that death is not the end of this unfolding of the presence of our incarnate God. Graced evolution continues, maybe forever. We seem to have forgotten the hints and glimpses given to us over fifty years ago in the Vatican II document *Lumen Gentium*. For instance in paragraph 48: "Then will come the time of the restoration of all things in Christ (Acts 3: 21). Then the human race, as well as the entire world... will be perfectly re-established in Christ." (Eph 1: 10) And again, in *Gaudium et Spes* we find another glimpse of an insight that would begin to captivate our imaginations and now permeates our spirituality with its correlation between divine love and the divine flow of Creation's evolution at every level of our most intimate, human and sacred lives; "God taught us that the new command of love was the basic law of human perfection *and hence of the world's transformation."* (par 38)

Julian of Norwich believed that every living thing will continue to flourish after death, eternally. Evolution, the work of the Holy Spirit, is always higher, deeper, still more 'magnanimous' (Pope Francis), ever-moving and inexorably drawn towards that infinite horizon of divine completion. We are but beginning this infinite exploration, a journey that has scarcely started, and our young eyes are as yet unaccustomed to the guiding light of revelation, distracted and seduced like children by all kinds of doubts, lesser gods and counter-attractions; by a lack of faith education and a loving community. Above all, by ignorance of the universal human stain we all carry: that strange and powerful fascination with darkness, destruction and evil.

You won't find these meditations in the doctrines of a catechism; you'll find them in the tabernacle of your own heart, beating with divine and aching devotion – a heart that believes in its God-given beauty and wisdom. So trust it. You must open it to your graced imagination. Let its creativity flow free with the pulsing energy of the Holy Creative Spirit that animates and powers all life, and is honoured and adored by all mainstream religions and cultures. And why am I writing to you like this? Because, even though I've never fretted too much about what happens to me after I die, much preferring to leave it all in the hands of my divine Lover, I find an excitement within me about what I soon may be enjoying. I'm strangely captivated by all kinds of possibilities. This is a comfort that distracts me from a sense of total loss, and draws me to those shutters of wonder that open onto panoramas of unimaginable and breathtaking beauty and welcome. And my secret hope is that in your own hour of need you may find unexpected graces to hold you, as you ponder these divine words of pure love and being. Rabindranath Tagore's poem always rings a bell in my heart:

I thought that my voyage had come to its end
at the last limit of my power; that the path before me was closed,
that provisions were exhausted
and the time come to take shelter in a silent obscurity.
But I find that thy will knows no end in me.
And when old words die out on the tongue,
new melodies break forth from the heart;
and where the old tracks are lost,
new country is revealed with its wonders.[57]

✿ 76 ✿

BECOMING LOVE

It is only love that enables me, even momentarily, to face my own powerless, helpless fragility just now, to face the fire of what is surely destroying me, to openly engage with my continuing diminishment into death. As this deadly but hopefully transforming process burns through my body and mind, I try to make sense of my weakness and fear. It seems that God's love does not protect me from anything, but somehow enables me, strengthens and supports me in the midst of the dying I'm enduring. This is Incarnation in practice. My pain *is* the fleshed and very tangible presence of God living in me, of his incarnate love reminding me every moment of his intimate intertwining in the very fibres of my body. It somehow manages to touch with courage, patience, even tenderness those hurting places, cauterising everything that is not love. Until only love is left. And it still surprises me that each of you, dear steadfast readers, will one day have to undergo this same journey, dance, work, give or take a step or two, before you die.

And in the end, it sometimes seems to me now, that is the ultimate goal: to become love; for this shrinking, dying body *to be* love in the world. Love is where we've come from and it is our destiny. It is who you truly are, and who I am too. It is our deepest truth. The only sin is the absence of love in us. But to love purely and unconditionally is very different from what we usually think it is! Jesus said to Peter "You must be ground like wheat, and once you have recovered, then you can turn and help your brothers and sisters." (Lk 22: 31-32) It seems as though you can only truly love and help others along their lives' awkward paths as far as you have endured your own experience of agony.

There is another dimension of this fullness of loving, this final surrender to the Creator's heart, this falling in love with a personal lover. I write of the God I believe is revealed as the ground of being, as the artist of beauty, as the cosmic consciousness, as the highest vibration of the love-energy that makes evolution happen, as the very epicentre of the mystery of my being. But, people ask, can you actually fall in love with such abstractions? How can you give your human heart to a universal presence which is spread across all Creation? This question touches on the core of Incarnation. In Jesus, God gave us a human body and heart that we could humanly love to the fullest. John's wonderful words are never far from my mind where he rapturously delights in an incarnate, human, physical God: "Something which has existed from the beginning, that we have heard, and we have seen with our own eyes; that we have watched and touched with our hands, the Word who is life..."(1 John 1: 1-4) Twice more he repeats these words with great delight.

The above question demands a more complete response. It takes us into the central significance of Incarnation, of Christianity, of 'the Faith'. This significance, this revelation is that, because in the fleshing of God, when we love and serve another truly and compassionately, then this is what we mean by loving God too. Remember the thrust of our retreats, writing and discussions of the past decades: their one relentless aim was to deepen our understanding of Incarnation – that when we love another we are loving God, that our human love is divine love incarnate, that human love does not need another 'better and higher octane' kind of heavenly intensity – there's only the one authentically true human love – just like the love of Jesus who was like us in all things except sin. To love God more, and personally, here and now, the only way for Christians is to intensify, purify and spread our love for each and every creature in our world; especially those we find most difficult. *Our personal love of God is the same as our love and forgiveness for the least of those in our lives. Achieving this is the ultimate death, and preparation for it.* All of this is something that is burning into my soul with a greater intensity than ever as I move into a darker, yet brighter place.

There are many ways of trying to understand, trying to express, trying to cope with this astonishing mystery, this same truth in a more mystical manner. Christian mystics speak of being spellbound by the divine face, of falling in love with the face of Jesus. Richard Rohr writes of the "early mirroring we receive from our parents as being particularly important". The adoring gaze, the look of love. James Finley develops this image. He believes that when God eases us out of God's heart onto this planet, God searches for a place that is most like paradise, and this is the mother's gaze. In the mother's gaze, she transparently sacramentalises God's infinite gaze, looking into the eyes of the infant. And when the infant looks into her eyes it is looking into God's eyes, incarnate in and *as* her mother's loving eyes. And so, as always, we are back to the wonder of the Incarnation again. Please remember the depth and healing power in these teachings: there are not two loves, two kinds of forgiveness, two levels or depths of wonder – there's only the one – but there are many levels of understanding and acceptance of that *unum necessarium*, that vital incarnational way of being, of seeing, and of loving. When we imbibe that unity between the human and the divine in our mother's arms, all other loves will flow from it. *To be truly human in all our endeavours is to be truly divine in them too.*

Fyodor Dostoyevsky puts it so clearly: "Love people even in their sin, for this is the semblance of Divine Love and is the highest love on earth. Love all God's creation, the whole and every grain of sand in it. Love every leaf, every ray of God's light. Love the animals, love the plants, love everything. If you love everything, you will perceive the divine mystery in things... And you will come at last to love the whole world with an all-embracing love."[58]

$ 77 $

PERFECT WEAKNESS

One of the fears I carry in the event of these thoughts and rumina-
tions ever becoming public, is that they would be seen as the bleatings
and whimpering of an old fool, a cowardly wimp unable to take
his beating like a man. (In a weird kind of way I feel I'm trying to
exorcise me before I go, all that's deeply flawed and hidden in my
make-up; to smash the wall of false appearance and pretence that
lies at the sick heart of my inherited clericalism.) But also, I would
not like to be remembered as a coward. Since, because of the fear I
often feel, I've always prayed for courage, and prized it as the queen
of graces. I'm aware that when discussing the core of spirituality,
of engraced humanity, that the presence of fragility, failure, falling,
inner confusion is always emphasised. Without this poverty of spirit
we dangerously and continually miss the whole point of salvation:
the suffering, the cross, the death of the ego, the weakness mentioned
so often by St Paul. Pick up any of our reliable and authentic guides to
wholeness, to holiness, to Christlikeness, and this message is unfail-
ingly the first and last foundation of the spiritually mature person.
Miss out on that part (and how we all strive to do that!) and we're
living in a fool's paradise.

So what makes a person truly human? Is it the anxious, unfinished soul like mine, the restless heart, unsure, incomplete, utterly
needy, ego-driven? Or is it the person in charge of herself, confident,
composed and at peace? Writers, including Fr Ronald Rolheiser and
Michael Buckley SJ, have offered an example. They have written about
Socrates and Jesus in terms of human excellence. They pointed out
that Socrates went to his death with calmness and poise. He accepted
the judgement of the court, spoke about his impending decision,

found no cause for fear, unwaveringly reached for the poison, courageously drank it and died with dignity. There was no panic, no scene, no hesitation, no emotion and no tears, only composure, self-awareness and assurance. Jesus, however, was much to the contrary. Almost hysterical with terror and fear, Jesus searched for the comfort of his friends, wept, shed blood, cried out in isolation from the cross. "I am forsaken, forsaken. O God, my God, have you forsaken me too?"

Buckley and Rolheiser believe that Jesus was a more profoundly weak man than Socrates. Socrates never wept over Athens as Jesus did Jerusalem (Lk 19: 41). His hand and face were sure when he drank the hemlock. He never expressed sorrow and pain at the betrayal of his friends. He was possessed and integral, never over-extended, always in command of himself, convinced that the just man could never suffer genuine hurt. Socrates, one of the greatest men who ever lived, a paradigm of what humanity can achieve, was a magnificent philosopher with a marvellous mind. Jesus, emotionally torn, incessantly suffering, driven by inner and unseen emotions that were always close to his skin, was a salvific human being, with a big heart, open to God.

Rolheiser points out that "In Socrates there was, certainly in the face of death, a poise, an ease, an interior peace, and an attractive calm that was absent in Jesus". Socrates always looked attractive; Jesus did not. Jesus sweated blood, shed tears he was unable to hide, and was stripped naked and humiliated in front of his loved ones. It is not easy to look good on wood. How I fear looking awful, slurring and slipping, powerless to lessen my neediness and fragility. No longer able to protect myself from pain, I fear the loss of control over my life, the humiliation of having to ask for the most basic everyday needs. I want to be 'cool' like Socrates who died alone, not weakly human and begging for company like Jesus.

I suppose Rolheiser is saying that by protecting ourselves from weakness we do not ever become vulnerable enough to enter into a healing, saving relationship with anyone. He goes on to say it is better to be sensitive and vulnerable than to be severe and unfeeling, and ends his article: "It's better to be sad than bitter, better to be hurting than hard, better to taste death than never risk living, better to feel rejection than never to have loved, better to shed tears than be indifferent, better to groan in interior anguish than to prematurely resolve tension, to sometimes look the fool, the needy one, the simpleton, than to always successfully hide what's most true inside us, so as to be the one who never has a hair, a feeling, or an opinion that's out of place."[59]

There's an aspect of the invincible courage of the vulnerable Jesus that delights my heart: his readiness to break the Scriptures open for our benefit. What inner authority was springing up inside to enable him to declare "The Law says... but I say."? He openly disagrees with the Scriptures in many places. He consistently flouts a long list of seemingly sacred taboos, and suffers for his trouble. He reduces six hundred and thirteen clear biblical commandments down to two – love of God and love of neighbour; but now these are not two but one. He omits troublesome verses with which he does not agree. He does it also to defend people. He was accused of preaching 'mere humanism' or 'situation ethics'. He feels free to interpret the Law. In the Sermon on the Mount he repeats six times "The Law says... but I say". When we can read the holy book like that, with the heart's ears, we are listening to a voice deeper than our own; we are in tune with our inner and divine authority. We are asking the ultimate questions such as "How do you go about losing your little life to find the bigger one?"[60]

Sometimes these observations around the humanity, the weakness and vulnerability of Jesus (above) bring some peace, meaning and consolation to me. When I cannot think straight or find peace, cannot sit down, lie down, or stop crying, when I wonder if I can manage another twenty-four hours, then I find some comfort in the extraordinarily broken face of the human Jesus as the perfect face of God. When I despair at how little of real worth I have achieved, when I remember how even those accomplishments that I have managed have been ruined by self-interest and a well-disguised ego, I find a mercy, a lambent light in the weakness of Jesus. "For because he himself has suffered and been tempted, he is able to help those who are tempted (Heb 2: 18)... For we do not have a high priest who is unable to sympathise with our weaknesses, but who *in every respect* has been tempted as we are (Heb 4: 15)... since he himself is beset with weakness." (Heb 5: 2) I mentioned my dismay at how my suffering closes me to the pain of others to my editorial friend, Caroline. She replied: "'My God, my God, why have you forsaken me?' gives a consoling insight into the humanity of Jesus. He who had been so moved by the suffering of others, when in extremis himself found he was closed to the pain of anyone else, as are you, for he calls out 'me' not 'us'. He was concerned only for himself at that moment, not for the two men on either side or for his distraught mother looking up at him, who were also feeling forsaken. So, my friend, do not beat yourself up!"

❦ 78 ❦

A LOVE CALLED CANCER

It's a few months since I last wrote to you, dear tumour. You have not taken my advice about any of the issues I raised. No matter. What I want to mention here are a few of the ways you have unexpectedly enriched my life, and for which, while there is still time, I wish to thank you. I never prayed for your annihilation, for your banishment from my life. How could I? Any sentence of the Gospel would point to your unique and vital power to transform my soul. During those terrible nights and days of loss and pain, I somehow became more conscious of new truths stirring deeply within me. Here are a few purely random examples. As the truth of my departure from this life becomes more obvious, and as I finally begin to accept that profound reality, unsuspected and timely patterns of awareness deepen. I thank you, dear tumour, for the following:

A PLACE FOR GRACE:

Kathleen Dowling, a hospice worker and psychotherapist who died in 2017, noticed a graced shimmering and often a palpable transformation in consciousness around many of the people she had accompanied through their approaching death experience. This was like a subtle but profound movement from the edge to the centre of their souls; a dimension of awareness and inner being, from preconceived tragedy to experienced blessing. It was like the possibility of entering the radiance of one's Essential Nature, a conscious re-merging with the Ground of our Being from which we all once unconsciously emerged. I read all of this with an intense focus. It seemed like a heavily disguised space for grace in my current and future suffering surrender.

It happens, Kathleen wrote, "between the terror of the impending loss of our separate, personal selves, and the experience of a transformed consciousness of wider, deeper Belonging and Unity".

Those of us who have pastorally ministered to the dying will know that sometimes it can be an astonishingly swift and radical death and rebirth. I remember reading a passage from theologian Karl Rahner where he wrote about this moment. He believed that there is no such thing in the world or in our hearts as a literal vacancy, a vacuum. "And whatever space is really left by death, by parting, by apparent emptiness, by separation – there is God."

LIKE A BIRD ON A WIRE:

The beloved Leonard Cohen has sung about the freedom he had sought all his life. "Like a bird on a wire, like a drunk in a midnight choir, I have tried, in my way, to be free." So have we all, I suppose – from the baby trying to establish its individuality, separateness and personhood by saying no, to the old woman or man in the nursing home, doing the same thing. Each new day a pure gift from God, a bonus of newness. Every experience of my senses, now a deeper experience. The freedom of being unframed at last, of seeing and sensing without borders, a unique opportunity for pure awareness, unencumbered by the normal pressures, demands, responsibilities, anxieties of the past decades. Maybe this is why I so love Rumi's lines: "Out beyond ideas of right and wrong there's a field; I'll meet you there." Without your arrival, dear tumour, I would never have found, or even glimpsed, that special bright field. I would never be able to truly see, to become untwisted enough in my soul to recognise the divine beauty of my deepest being.

THE GRACE OF NOW:

"To accept death is to accept God" wrote well known contemplative and author Thomas Keating. "The Ground of Being" is how philosopher and theologian Paul Tillich (d 1965) identified God (Act 17: 28).

We desire to be in that free place yet we fear it also. Being in that spacious post-death ground of my being will set me free. Yet, as you can see, I run from it. But it is where love is limitless and always unconditional. I can only guess what that experience is like, so different from our constricted, painfully evolving existence here on Earth of Love and Being. And so, as a friend Anne Marie reminded me in an email this morning of a note she made at one of our last retreats, "Live your life to the last beat of your pulse" and a quote from John O'Donohue, "The unlived life is the great tragedy". Dear tumour, because of you I can try to live my life as abundantly as possible 'to the last beat of my pulse'. Not everyone gets that blessed opportunity.

ALREADY SACRED:

The Christ of the Incarnation is present whenever and wherever the material and the spiritual co-exist as one. "Everything is already christened," writes Richard Rohr, "all anointing, blessing, declaring and baptising is just to help us get the point!" The point being that everything and everyone is already anointed and blessed by virtue of its being created in the womb of our fertile Earth, of our ever-birthing Mother-God. We bless water, for instance, not to make it holier; the very source of life and evolution, the most beautiful of divine creations, how can we make it any holier? Similarly with all the sacraments. According to Rahner, celebrating the sacraments adds nothing to human nature and its qualities; they reveal and witness to the holiness and divinity of what always and already is at the heart of our lives. Like the bread at the Eucharist, the water at Baptism, human love at Marriage. Like spring to the renewing of the land and of our hearts after the winter of waiting; like the energy and delight in the body and eyes of the growing baby; like the universal healing that floods through everything, bringing a harvest of fullness to fields and limbs and stars. We desperately need all these rites, rituals, sacraments, sacramentals, blessings because, in our finiteness, weakness and ignorance we keep forgetting (or maybe were never told about the real redeeming meaning of) Incarnation: that all is always and already graced beyond measure, that my tumour is to me what his cross was to Jesus, no more no less.

THE TWO SELVES:

We have often mentioned the True Self and the False Self in these pages. This kind of distinction is very helpful in our pursuit of spiritual maturing, of the complexities of befriending our authentic, complicated selves. Nobody writes of the faces and peculiarities of these twins within the womb of every soul with the authority and sure-footedness of Richard Rohr who has walked with us through the pages of this book. While experiencing many glimpses of these two inhabitants during the past six months, one in particular will become, I feel sure, a useful and powerful blessing in the months ahead. She, the True Self, sees the False Self as our 'cosy image' of ourselves - individual, distinct and separate from the rest of life, independent and self-assured, in charge of our own destinies because we have earned them, deserved them, merited them by our 'good and religious deeds' all our lives.

Therefore we are terrified of dying. All our resources and motivations come from this lifetime and its successes, from this individual world, as though we would live here forever. Self-constructed, shallow and inwardly fearful, it seeks to hide the fact that this life is passing away and there will be nothing left. Therefore, without vision or depth of thinking, death becomes the enemy. "The False Self has no substance," writes Rohr, "no permanence, no vitality, only various forms of immediate gratification." Everything goes into staving off the bitter day, clinging in desperation to every means of staying alive. The False Self knows nothing of the soul. How do you feel as you read these words?

Most of us belong to the community of Jesus that tries to protect us from going down that road which is a temptation for everyone. Even for Jesus. The final destination of the road less travelled is not a nihilistic mirage of nothingness, but an attractive wholeness: the intimacy and union with the Love that created us, and sustains us, and that is already at home in us. I will meditate on the deeper meaning of this mystery every day for the rest of my life. My True Self is the Risen Christ in me, the Spirit of eternal mercy, the God of unconditional love. Knowing this, how can one fear death. Nothing real is lost in death.

Death, in fact is the only gateway, the necessary pathway of pain to the glory for which we are created. We do not walk through those open gates alone. We are already utterly connected; not just connected but we have become the very essence of the Creator of life and death. There is no separation, as I will keep insisting to myself from now on; I am part of everything created. "Enlightenment, for an ocean-wave," wrote Thich Nhat Hanh, "is the moment the wave realises that it is water. At that moment, all fear of death disappears."[61] Only my False Self will die at the end of my human life: my real life, my True Self, already at home in everlasting love, will return to that space, place and playground that it once knew so well. Life does not really end, as so many of our funeral rites remind us; it simply changes form, Rohr assures us, and "continues evolving into ever new shapes and forms of beauty". Only since meeting you, dear tumour, have I had the chance to meet the essential nature of my True Self. And to become, before I die, the fleshed reality of the Love called God.

THE UNFINISHED SYMPHONY:

In a weird way all my life I've been very aware of the incompleteness of everything. Nothing was enough. I always wanted more. (Spare me giving embarrassing examples!) Then I came across this gem of a paragraph by the beloved spiritual writer Henri Nouwen, a Dutch priest. With time ticking away for me now, a precious time when a vague awareness can assume fine edges and a sharp focus, this seemed to bring its own kind of relief and completeness: "Our life is a short time in expectation, a time in which sadness and joy kiss each other at every moment. There is a quality of sadness that pervades all the moments of our lives. It seems that there is no such thing as a clear-cut pure joy, but that even in the most happy moments of our existence we sense a tinge of sadness. In every satisfaction, there is an awareness of limitations. In every success, there is the fear of jealousy. Behind every smile, there is a tear. In every embrace, there is loneliness. In every friendship, distance. And in all forms of light, there is the knowledge of surrounding darkness... But this intimate experience in which every bit of life is touched by a bit of death can point us beyond the limits of our existence. It can do so by making us look forward in expectation to the day when our hearts will be filled with perfect joy, a joy that no one shall take away from us."[62] Maybe this is God's ways of reminding us not to get settled too soon! Don't forget the mountain you were born to climb! With you around, dear tumour, there is no chance of that happening!

JE NE REGRETTE RIEN:

You may remember, dear reader, my fairly regularly expressed fear of dying still disturbed by significant regrets, one of them being my deep anxiety about spending the last days of my life tormented by the same fear that kept me from living the abundant life. I have used lists of examples collected from the notes of carers of the dying to make the point about doing all we can to avoid dying in this regrettable frame of mind. My particular concern was that those last days of my life – maybe the very time I now have left – would be darkly marked by the fear I usually carry, and that it might prevent me from saying, doing or writing the truth of my heart.

This was usually related to the clerical institution of which I am an unavoidable part. There's the rub! It is not the Church, the loving and free community gathered together by Jesus, the Human One, that frustrates, deeply disappoints, and frequently enrages committed Christianity; it is the closed, clerical and too often destructive Institution. However, while I will never be seen as a Dan Berrigan, a Dorothy Day, an Edward Schillebeeckx, a de Chardin, I have, in my own small way, tried to tell my truth. I have of course suffered for that; the soulless and fearful Institution always bites back. (You may have your own list of those faithful writers persecuted for their work, even, and especially, during the last few decades. Many of them friends of mine, I know they suffered deeply, unnecessarily and undefended.) But for me the sense of freedom was, and still is, immense. Like all of us, I suppose, I just wanted to make a difference by emphasising the astonishing, felt reality of God's unconditional love. The Buddhists teach you to say or write it, and then you let it go into the hands of the Spirit of Life. And you resolve to keep doing this with peace in your heart.

One last word here. There is a final all-embracing vision, a conviction that holds, sustains my courage in mornings and evenings of fear. It is happening these very days. It is a kind of gradually-forming vision, a perspective, a radical paradigm shift. It is very like the way Spring delicately moves into our fields, allotments and cities with beautiful feet, or is glimpsed now here, now there, until one day we know it will stay. Put another way, the day will come when, like rain falling on parched land, like light filtering in through utter darkness, like life slowly returning to a stricken land, you will find a wonderful awareness warming your soul. It is the moment you know for sure, that the birth and death of everything, the sustaining and empowering of all that works towards good, the precious energy that creates, heals and quickens our souls - is LOVE. It invades me like the dawn. It brings the deepest sigh. Once sensed, the precipice of despair will always remain out of reach. All of this is old hat; we've been told it since our nursery years. And one day, sooner or later, it sits forever at the altar table of our hearts.

❧ 79 ❧

WHEN IS IT TIME TO GO?

I have read about the death of many saints, and been surprised at their bargaining with God about delaying the moment of departure. They begged for extra time to wait for a last word with a friend arriving from afar. Or to make sure they had completed their penances for the sins of their lives. Or to make peace with an old enemy with whom they wished to be reconciled before leaving. Even one of our companions throughout these pages, Teilhard de Chardin, had two requests – he wanted more time to finish his last book, and to hang on until Easter Sunday – and our compassionate God agreed. In spite of such wishes, they would all, I think, be fairly convinced that death would hold something utterly surprising and dramatic.

Fr Joseph Boyle, an elderly monk from St Benedict's Monastery in Colorado, was asked about his expectations at the time of his death. "Yes, I expect death to be a transition. I think it is a movement into a space that is not limited by our bodies and our senses that are quite limited now... we'll relate to people and the beauty of who they are without the ego-agendas we have right now. I see life after death as infinite love... it strikes me as a homecoming with all the sisters and brothers... I certainly have a very deep hope that it is a transition into an incredible life."[63] How do you see this mystery, dear reader? We know so little about this momentous happening. Maybe the relentless business of living prevents us from spending much time thinking about it. And maybe that's just as well!

When asked if he believed there would be a transformation at death, Fr Thomas Keating, who died just a few months ago (2018), and who was a dear friend of Fr Joseph's, replied, "Death is only a part of the process of living... It is not an occasion for only sorrow, but an occasion of rejoicing that our friends and relatives have moved to a deeper level of union... It is not we who are really dying but only the ego-driven false self that is experiencing the end of its illusory life... (For the true self) eternal life means perfect happiness without space or time limitations... It is spaciousness itself. And it is already within you. It involves freedom from the senses and our thinking processes; in other words entering into the simplicity of the divine energy that pours itself out into the world through continuing creation and all stages of consciousness."[64]

Here we have two deeply holy contemplatives. They are trying to understand and keep the intrinsic, invisible connection between this life and the next. Keating adds: "We are always connected to God and each other and every living being. Most of us just do not realise it. Jesus prays that we can see things in their unity and wholeness... There is only One Love that will lead and carry us across when we die. If we are already at home with Love here, we will quite literally move into heaven, Love's eternal home. Death is not a changing of worlds, as most imagine, as much as the walls of this world infinitely expanding."[65]

The most useful way in which we can contribute to the unfolding of an evolving humanity and universe in accordance with the divine will, is by increasing the pure energy of love at every moment of our lives. We put love where there was no love before. The next big breakthrough in the story of our evolving world, is the creation of more love, to spread it, to become it. It is the main implication of the Incarnation. And the first responsibility of the Community of Jesus, is to remember, preach and practise that loving vision.

Love alone provides the current response to the needs of desperate people in a warring world. Churches, governments, local communities will all do their necessary best. But that will never be enough. Creation has a heart of love because its Creator has. We must evolve the energy of love, learn it and spread it. It is something we can all do in many different ways – openly within our communities and hiddenly in our hearts – advancing, enhancing and completing the work of Creation, of Evolution, of the Kingdom of God. But without each one's lifelong effort to become a sacrament, a symbol, a fleshing of incarnate love, the whole beautiful dream of God for us and for the universe will spin out of orbit leaving a terrible and nihilistic dark hole. This way of seeing, of being, of thinking has, I hope, permeated the pages of this book. And with my last breath it will be my deepest desire to diminish and die into that eternal love.

Reflecting on these huge issues occupies my mind with increasing intensity but not with increasing anxiety. In fact it brings me some comfort because it is all positive, hopeful, based on the supremacy of love. These thoughts remind me not to get stuck in my grief, that the work of the tumour is to dislodge all lesser and negative distractions that drag and drain me from the one, last and definitive focus. All of this is an unending struggle with the shadow, the ego, the human stain. "...but if we lean into the pain, and move to its rhythm," James Finley reminds us, "love charts its own course and brings us to a profound understanding of this final letting go."[66]

✤ 80 ✤

SLOW DAWN

We are in our last Reflection now, the last lap. May I mention yet one more healing moment? As you will have noticed, I could be accused of wallowing in self-pity and victimhood. 'Is there any sorrow like mine?' And now, six months later, as I weigh up my black cloud with a greater sense of perspective and objectivity, I clearly see how wrong I was. I honestly now see my situation as very low on the scale of intense pain. Haven't I heard so many terrible stories myself in the course of the decades of my ministries? I'm deeply grateful for getting that obvious truth right. What has always struck me as one of the most piercing and enduring experiences of pain is that of a mother's loss of her child. I cannot, of course, even vaguely, know anything about this experience, only look in from the outside. I have watched mothers in parish congregations with the pain of a lost child etched into their faces for many decades, probably forever. A quick death and a very slow resurrection. Even in my callow days of unforgivable ignorance, I have silently wondered at the mysterious, inexplicable and seeming eternal bond, oneness, and the utterly profound identity that motherhood creates.

Mirabai Starr works with Richard Rohr in New Mexico. The death of her beloved fourteen-old daughter Jenny, in a car crash, was "an avalanche" she wrote, "annihilating everything in its path". In her book *God of Love* she tells us how she was "plunged into the abyss, instantly dropped into the vast stillness and pulsing silence... so shattered I could not see my own hand in front of my face". She wrote about the various spiritual experiences that visited her by way of consolation; a "sacred emptiness... a holy longing", and added "I hated them all. I didn't want vastness of being. I wanted my baby back... But

I discovered there was nowhere to hide when radical sorrow unravelled the fabric of my life. I could rage against the terrible unknown – and I did, for I am human and have this vulnerable body, passionate heart and complicated mind – or I could turn toward the cup, bow to the Cupbearer, and say 'Yes'."

Mirabai explained how, in the acceptance of the cup she softened into her pain and yielded to her suffering. And as this process began to grow stronger, she found that a compassion for all beings began to swell in her heart. Have you noticed that deepening, dear reader, at any time in your life, when your own heartbreak opened you to the tears of another? This widening of her mercy, this profound stripping by grief, drew her towards the shattered souls of many. "I became acutely aware of my connectedness to mothers everywhere who had lost children, who were, at this very moment, hearing the impossible news that their chid had died..."[67]

Quaker Parker J Palmer is a true teacher and another hero of mine. His books are many, his last being *On the Brink of Everything: Grace, Gravity and Getting Old*. "As I weather the late autumn of my own life," he writes, "I find nature a trustworthy guide." He describes himself as a 'professional melancholic' whose sadness every autumn arose from the certain and imminent death of summer's beauty. This sadness prevented him enjoying any of the "sensuous delights" of the fall. Then one season he began to understand the whole natural process at a deeper level. In a kind of resurrection moment he saw the hidden, perennial promise disguised by the passing death. The abundance of seeds and the composted leaves were all busy, out of sight, even in the harshest winter, preparing the world for another rising, another greening, another spring. For Parker it was autumn days. We all wait for the moment, profound or seemingly flimsy, graced or seemingly 'natural', when the penny drops and the bigger picture fills our souls completely. As it did his. And as it is doing mine. All, indeed, is grace.

You may remember, dear reader, my telling you about the morning of my cancer news, how I felt as though a large STOP! sign had suddenly appeared before the rest of my life and its plans. Palmer refs to a ROAD CLOSED! sign that at first seemed to be an irredeemable disaster, but forced him, eventually, to search for another way – nature's way – the Christian would say the Easter way. Palmer writes, "Perhaps death possesses a grace that we who fear dying, who find it ugly and even obscene, cannot see: that dying itself, as devastating as we know it can be, contains the hope of a certain beauty."

The theme of the depth in everything if we have the eyes to see it (the oak in the acorn, the saint in the sinner, the divine in the speck of dust) runs through the thought of Palmer, the insights of the nature mystics, the pages of the Gospel and of this book. Incarnation is already written large into every human heart at birth. Simply to be is already to have the dream. All Creation has its hidden wholeness. Palmer's eyes were opened at the deepest levels. "Though I still grieve as beauty goes to ground, autumn reminds me to celebrate the primal power that is forever making all things new in me, in us, and in the natural world."[68] And the natural world, we know, is God incarnate.

ONE WORD OF TRUTH

As the days unfold, when freedom from pain lets my spirit free to remember, to relive and to wonder at the twists and turns of my life, I notice a disturbing and recurring thought pattern emerging. I have mentioned this already. I wish to do so again. It seems to me that I was so conscious of a culture of hiding, of cover-up, of fear at practically every level of my life: personally, priestly, in seminary, at home, in parishes, with the neighbours, with colleagues and parishioners. Conversations of meaning, of openness, of trust, of mutual exploration about doubts, relationships, dreams, personal spirituality or heart-breaking situations were almost entirely just not on. So many communications, wherever they happened, were guarded, shallow and ring-fenced with fear. This situation, in a so-called family of God's love, in a community of Jesus' compassion, beggars belief. I feel it crushed my soul.

I think I held on to my basic graced nature, my family selfhood, through the humanity of laypeople, of women and men whom I trusted and with whom I could be 'myself'; also through my visits to other lands to work, study and experience fresh communities; but especially in the company of all those genuinely searching, suffering and utterly authentic souls I trusted and shared with in the many retreats of my life. In such places there are no masks. I have no doubt whatever that many will say I'm all wrong about this. 'His soul has got twisted, bitter.' Maybe not. My soul, in fact, was never so clear and calm as it is tonight. From the beginning I clarified that I was only writing about what was filling my heart during these final days of darkness. And yet, these have been the very times when truth has emerged, slowly, shyly but relentlessly, powerfully and invincibly.

Paradoxically, even with such blessed insight, as I write now it occurs to me that this was exactly what both Jesus, in his condemnation of anything pharisaical, and Pope Francis mean when they get so angry about the cursed culture of power. And the culture of clericalism now permeates the Institution of the Catholic Church to its very core, bringing shame on the most powerful, from the West of Ireland to the heart of Rome. Only a fool would quibble with the truth of what is now hurting me so much; only the deliberately blind are still in denial.

A small and recent example of a moment of personal presence and beautiful truth that I long for comes to me now. It happened at a final meeting I had with Mr A, a senior consultant at the Aintree Hospital last week. We knew the game was up, the chips were down, the writing on the wall was clear. "How are you?" the consultant asked me. "I'm dying," I said. He looked at me keenly. "Well, I am, am I not?" There was no self-pity, only a statement of fact. Pure truth. No more talk of a cure, of opting for another line of chemotherapy. Mr A, deeply moved, as was I, seemed to sense the holiness of the moment. In the silence that followed, the atmosphere in the room and the depth of awareness in its occupants – a stoma nurse, a student nurse, my friend Margaret, Mr A and myself – seemed to change. There was a stillness in all of us. It was a rare kind of encounter when two people enter that liminal space where something mystical and transforming happens. And our eyes were moist. "I trust in my blessed humanity," I said, "in my engraced life." Mr A and I looked at each other for a long moment. "Every time you leave my clinic," he said, "I sit and think about you. I am humbled at your courage. Thank you."

Later, in the hospital café, Margaret and I struggled to do the impossible - to recreate the moment. We spoke of a presence, the power and physicality of it, the healing and redemption of it. Here was a man, commanding huge respect and authority, becoming vulnerable before the four of us, a big man with a big heart, with complete and graced presence, reaching to bless me on my way – the same human/divine presence that God's own self revealed as the real and raw material of our truest lives and selves. I asked Margaret about her version of what had happened. "An unusual atmosphere of trust was created," she replied. "It was no longer about patient and doctor, priest and consultant. There were no more roles here, no more masks, but a man-to-man integrity, a real encounter with affection, dignity and a respect able to bear enough truth to set you both free. You seemed to bless each other with the silent power of your presence, your trusting gaze, and we all felt it." Nothing too extraordinary I suppose. A bit egotistical for me, perhaps. However, a moment of utter truth lasts forever. And you cannot expect it every day. But neither can you live without it for long.

AFTERWORD

Those words for the last reflection were first scribbled here in my flat on 31st December 2018. The end of the year: the end of the book? Yet that very night, as the New Year's bells rang out in the distance, I was back in bed six of bay three in Aintree Hospital suffering from unforeseen complications – as if I needed any more evidence of the unpredictable vicissitudes of my life!

Discharged five days later on the eve of my birthday, I carried with me the news that the CT scans now indicated a lifespan of six months or so. Maybe more; probably less. The palliative care consultant had gently advised me to do the things I longed to do, to spend time with family and friends and to put my affairs in order.

Now, after a week at home, I have decided to end *Dancing to my Death* while listening to Mozart: the nearest human experience to that mystical moment when nature and grace, heaven and earth meet most truly, according to Pope Benedict and his favourite theologian Hans Urs von Balthasar. Leonie and Mike, my dearest friends, have sent me wonderful homemade CDs to keep me company.

Gradually, everything somehow is becoming more simple and just fading away. We grow, and we die, by subtraction. Is that all there is? So why do I refer to the approach of death as a dance?

You would know the secret of death.
But how shall you find it unless you seek it in the heart of life?
For life and death are one,
even as the river and the sea are one...
Only when you drink from the river of silence
shall you indeed sing.
And when you have reached the mountain top,
then you shall begin to climb.
And when the earth shall claim your limbs,
then shall you truly dance.[69]

POSTSCRIPT FOR DANIEL

On the morning of Sunday, 20th January 2019, I had arrived to find you extremely breathless, waiting for a call from the palliative care nurse. On checking your mobile, I discovered she had already called and left a message. There then began a seemingly interminable round of phone calls as all the emergency contact numbers immediately went to answerphone. Eventually, after an inordinately long wait for the NHS 111 helpline, I was advised that a doctor would phone in due course.

More waiting. Your breathing was not improving and the situation began to feel more desperate by the minute. Should I call 999 against your express wish? At that moment, like an angel of mercy, the palliative care nurse arrived, realised immediately the seriousness of your condition and called for ambulance support.

After six hours in A&E, a variety of blood tests, a CT scan, an x-ray, and constant heart rate and oxygen level monitoring, together with unfailing kindness and care from the nurses and doctors, the consultant came to speak with you. She had all the results back and it was stark news: "significant blood-clots on both lungs". In response to your request for a truthful prognosis, Dr S told you honestly and compassionately, that the time was now limited but that everything possible would be done to make sure you were comfortable. You told her you were not afraid of death.

After the consultant had gone, you asked me to write down this sentence: *"I've heard of deadlines but this is taking the biscuit."*

I asked why you wanted those words written down.

"I want to write," you then said to me, *"how the conversation with Dr S felt – one last piece for the book."*

You then asked me to write a short paragraph about the morning phone calls. *"No more than three sentences, keep it short."* (I've written more. Forgive me!)

In the limited conversation on the ward after that, you shared the important things that you would like to be done. We both believed, the nursing staff too, that there would at least be time for you to write your piece and maybe even go home.

Peacefully and trustingly, in the early hours of Monday, 21st January, you entered into the eternal embrace of LOVE.

We will never know quite how that end-piece would have read. From all that has gone before in this book of extraordinary courage and hard-won wisdom, we do know it would have revealed deep faith and the complete surrender of your life, your beautiful spirit, with utter *"confidence in Love itself"*.

At home in Rathmore, Co. Kerry Daniel's ashes were buried with his parents and his beloved brother Joseph. We sang the final farewell:

> *"And when you get the choice to sit it out or dance,*
> *I hope you dance,*
> *I hope you dance."*

Those of us who knew and loved you, were blessed, always, by your dancing heart.

Margaret Siberry

ACKNOWLEDGEMENTS

From the very first page of this book, Daniel has acknowledged how important you have been to him dear reader. Throughout his ministry in parishes, higher education, retreats and not least his writing, he has relied upon your support and encouragement, and never more so than over these last six months. You will have noticed how often he has mentioned receiving an email, a card, a call or a quote that gave him a lift on darker days. Thank you.

He would want to acknowledge especially the hours of dedicated editing, advice and support offered by his friend Caroline Weldon. As ever, Margaret Siberry has been there to affirm and encourage. A particular debt of gratitude is owed to Mags Gargan and the team at Columba. They had faith in Daniel to finish the book, whilst being fully aware of the fragility of his health.

Daniel has always been deeply aware of the encouragement to develop his creative talents he received from an early age from his family. Special thanks at this time go to his sister Maura and his brother Micheál whose love and support helped make him the wonderful person he became.

FOOTNOTES

FLYLEAF

1. William Stafford, *Ask Me:100 Essential Poems*, Graywolf Press, 1977, p 42

PART 1

REFLECTION 3

2. *The Essential Rumi: Childhood Friends*, Coleman Barks, with John Moyne, A.J. Arberry and Reynold Nicholson, New York, Harper One, 2004, p 142.

REFLECTION 8

3. Parker J. Palmer, *Let Your Life Speak: Listening for the Voice of Vocation*, Jossey-Bass, 2000, pp 2-3.

4. Richard Rohr, *Let Your Life Speak, Daily Meditation*, 27 May 2018, www.cac.org/let-your-life-speak-2018-05-27/

REFLECTION 9

5. David Whyte, *House of Belonging*, Many Rivers Press, 2002, p 23.

REFLECTION 10

6. Ursula King, *Pierre Teilhard de Chardin*, Orbis Books, 1999, p 53.

REFLECTION 11

7. ibid p 45.

8. ibid p 54.

REFLECTION 14

9. T.S. Eliot, *Four Quartets*, 'Little Gidding', Faber and Faber,1983, p 48, line 254.

10. op cit *Pierre Teilhard de Chardin*, p 53.

REFLECTION 15

11. ibid p 146.

12. ibid p 146-147.

13. ibid p 147.

14. ibid p 147-148.

15. Jean Vanier, *Befriending the Stranger*, Darton, Longman & Todd, 2005, p 87.

REFLECTION 17

16. Saki Santorelli, *Heal Thyself*, Crown Publications, 2000, p 80.

REFLECTION 20

17. ibid p 46.

PART 2

REFLECTION 21

18. Ruth Morrisey, *Sunday Independent,* 29 July 2018.

19. Gerry Andrews, *Sunday Independent,* 8 July 2018.

REFLECTION 26

20. Jean Vanier, *Be Not Afraid,* Griffin House, 1975, p 139.

REFLECTION 27

21. Carlo Carretto, *Love is for Living,* Darton, Longman &Todd, 1976, p 19.

REFLECTION 28

22. Rabbi Rami Shapiro, *Perennial Wisdom for the Spiritually Independent,* Skylight Paths, 2013, p xvi.

23. Richard Rohr, *Perennial Tradition: Weekly Summary,* 4 August 2018, www.cac.org/perennial-tradition-weekly-summary-2018-08-04/

REFLECTION 29

24. Donald Nicholl, *Holiness,* Darton, Longman & Todd, 1982, p 129.

25. ibid, pp 129-130.

REFLECTION 30

26. Henri Nouwen, *Here and Now: Living in the Spirit,* Darton, Longman & Todd, 1994, pp 69-70.

REFLECTION 31

27. Daniel O'Leary, *The Healing Habit,* Columba Press, 2016, p 75.

REFLECTION 32

28. Teilhard de Chardin, *Le Milieu Divin,* Fontana, 1964, pp 127-8.

29. *Rumi Selected Poems,* Penguin Books, 2004, p 109.

REFLECTION 34

30. Richard Rohr, *Questioning Our Loyalties, Daily Meditations,* 11 July 2018, www.cac.org/questioning-our-loyalties-2018-07-11/

REFLECTION 36

31. Saki Santorelli, *Heal Thyself,* Crown Publications, 2000, pp 109-110.

32. Derek Walcott, 'Love after Love' in *The Poetry of Derek Walcott 1948-2013,* Faber & Faber Ltd, 2014.

REFLECTION 37

33. Matthew Arnold, 'The Buried Life', *The Hundred Best Poems (Lyrical) In The English Language,* Selected by Adam L. Gowans, Gowans & Gray Ltd, 1904, p 4.

REFLECTION 39

34. R.S. Thomas, *Collected Poems: 1945-1990,* Phoenix Giants, 1993, p 533.

REFLECTION 40

35. Wallace Stevens, 'The Sail of Ulysses' from *Opus Posthumous,* Alfred A. Knopf, 1957.

PART 3

REFLECTION 42

36. Padraig J. Daly, *The Last Dreamers, New and Selected Poems*, Dedalus Press, 2008, p 103.

37. op cit *Heal Thyself*, p 166.

REFLECTION 44

38. Eithne Strong, *Spatial Nosing*, Salmon, 1993, p 85.

REFLECTION 45

39. op cit *The Healing Habit*, p 46.

REFLECTION 49

40. R.S. Thomas, *Collected Poems: 1945-1990*, Phoenix Giants, 1993, p 221.

REFLECTION 50

41. Ronald Rolheiser, 'Ode to the Church', *The Catholic Herald*, 13 September 2018, www.catholicherald.co.uk/magazine/an-ode-to-the-church/

REFLECTION 51

42. op cit *Heal Thyself*, p 173.

REFLECTION 52

43. op cit *Four Quartets*, 'Little Gidding', p 48.

REFLECTION 53

44. D.H. Lawrence, *Shadows in The Complete Poems*, Wordsworth Editions, 1994, p 613.

REFLECTION 55

45. Raymond Carver, *Poems for Life, Selected by Laura Barber*, Penguin Books, 2007, p 328.

REFLECTION 58

46. Dylan Thomas, *Selected Poems*, Penguin Classics, 2000, p 18.

REFLECTION 59

47. John Moriarty, *Nostos: An Autobiography*, The Lilliput Press, 2001, p 511.

PART 4

REFLECTION 66

48. Padraig Pearce, *Collected Works*, Phoenix Publishing, 1924, p 342.

REFLECTION 67

49. op cit *Love is for Living*, p 62.

REFLECTION 69

50. Richard Rohr, *Transforming Pain, Daily Meditation*, 17 Oct 2018, www.cac.org/transforming-pain-2018-10-17/

REFLECTION 70

51. Etty Hillesum, *An Interrupted Life and Letters from Westerbork*, Henry Holt, 1996, p 226.

52. ibid pp 29-31.

REFLECTION 71

53. Diarmuid O'Murchu, *Incarnation: A New Evolutionary Threshold*, Orbis Books, 2017, p 151.

REFLECTION 73

54. John Bate, *Damaged Beauty Needs a New Design*, The Gamecock Press, 1981, p 8.

55. Phoebe Hesketh, *The Leave Train, Enitharmon Press*, 1997, p 37.

REFLECTION 75

56. Brian Swimme, *The Universe is a Green Dragon*, Bear & Co., 1984, p 32.

57. Rabindranath Tagore, *Gitanjali*, Macmillan India, 1974, poem No 37, p 37.

REFLECTION 76

58. Fyodor Dostoyevsky, *The Brothers Karamazov*, Penguin Classics, 1972, p 375.

REFLECTION 77

59. Ronald Rolheiser, *Jesus' Sensitivity*, Article, 3 Oct 2004, www.ronrolheiser.com/jesus-sensitivity

60. Richard Rohr, *The Law Says...But I Say, Daily Meditation*, 10 January 2019, www.cac.org/the-law-says-but-I-say-2019.01.10

REFLECTION 78

61. Thich Nhat Hanh, *Living Buddha, Living Christ*, Riverhead Books, 1995, p 138.

62. Henri Nouwen, *Out of Solitude*, Ave Maria Press, 1974.

REFLECTION 79

63. Thomas Keating and Joseph Boyle with Lucette Verboven, *World Without End*, Bloomsbury 2017, p 148. © Thomas Keating and Joseph Boyle with Lucette Verboven, 2017, *World Without End*, Bloomsbury Continuum, an imprint of Bloomsbury Publishing Plc.

64. ibid p 87.

65. Thomas Keating, *Fruits and Gifts of the Spirit*, Lantern Books, 2007, p 89.

66. *Thomas Merton's Path to the Palace of Nowhere*, CD Sounds True, 2004, disc 5.

REFLECTION 80

67. Mirabai Starr, *God of Love: A Guide to the Heart of Judaism, Christianity and Islam*, Monkfish Book Publishing Company, 2012, pp 63-65.

68. Parker J Palmer, *On the Brink of Everything: Grace, Gravity and Getting Old*, Berrett-Koehler Publishers, 2018, pp 165-168.

AFTERWORD

69. Kahlil Gibran, *The Prophet*, Heinemann, 1972, pp 93-94.